Inv. to 121

ARTHUR COX 1891-1965

Arthur Cox 1891-1965

EUGENE McCAGUE

GILL & MACMILLAN

Published in Ireland by
Gill & Macmillan Ltd
Goldenbridge
Dublin 8
with associated companies throughout the world
© Eugene McCague 1994
0 7171 2194 1
Index compiled by Helen Litton
Print origination and design by Typeform Repro, Dublin
Printed by ColourBooks Ltd, Dublin

A catalogue record is available for this
book from the British Library.

1   3   5   4   2

To my mother

Contents

Acknowledgments

I received tremendous support from many people in the course of my research for this book. I am particularly indebted to Arthur Cox's step-daughters, Una O'Higgins-O'Malley who was a constant source of encouragement and of hospitality, and Mother Kevin who allowed me to draw on her memories of Arthur. Fr Roland Burke-Savage SJ had done some preliminary research on Arthur's life and generously gave me the results of his endeavours. Niall McLaughlin was an invaluable ally of Arthur in his professional career for over thirty years and provided a unique insight into life at 42 and 43 St Stephen's Green. I corresponded with and spent a marvellous afternoon in the company of the late Terence de Vere White, who provided me with countless colourful anecdotes in language so masterful that I have taken the liberty of transcribing many of them verbatim. John Donnelly provided stories, contacts and motivation in equally large measure and for his singular support in this and other ventures which I have undertaken I am deeply grateful.

As a complete novice at formal archival research I came to rely heavily on the staff at the National Archives and National Library and I thank them sincerely for their courtesy and forbearance. My special thanks are due to Fergal Altman, librarian at the firm of Arthur Cox, Seamus Helferty at the Archives Department of University College, Dublin, Fr Stephen Redmond SJ who is in charge of the Jesuit Archives, Bríd O'Brien at the library at Milltown Park and Margaret Byrne, librarian to the Incorporated Law Society.

My teachers at St Macartan's College in Monaghan imbued in me a great love of Irish history. This book provided a marvellous excuse to re-enter that world after an absence of many years. I was very honoured to have the opportunity to discuss my research with many distinguished historians and history-makers who, along with many friends of long standing, provided advice, encouragement and criticism, as appropriate. To the following I owe grateful appreciation: Kevin Anderson, Denis Bergin, Dr John Bowman, Fr Bruce Bradley SJ, Patrick Brennan, Dr Noël Browne, Tom Callan, Don Carroll, John

Carrigan, Frank Casey, Valerie de la Courte, Bishop James Corboy SJ, Mr Justice Declan Costello, Conor Crowley, Laurence Crowley, Niall Crowley, Judge Timothy Crowley, Dr Conor Cruise O'Brien, Dr Mary Daly, Patrick Dennis, Richard Dennis, Anthony Dudley, Dr Ronan Fanning, Oliver D. Gogarty SC, Lavinia Greacen, Mr Justice Frank Griffin, Gerard Harrison, Daire Hogan, Sean Hogan, Professor Gary Holbrook, Michael Holroyd, Professor Michael Hopkinson, Elizabeth Jameson, Peter Kelly SC, Justin Loughnane, John Lynch, Professor Patrick Lynch, Kevin McCourt, Paddy McGrath, James Maguire, Finbarr Madden, Dr F.O.C. Meenan, Jim Moloney, Mr Justice Thomas F. O'Higgins, Daniel O'Keeffe SC, Professor Eoin O'Malley, Fr Frank O'Neill SJ, Aodhagan O'Rahilly, Captain Mungo Park, Frank Plunkett-Dillon, Harry Robinson, Lord Shawcross, David Sheehy, Neil Smith, Gerard Torsney, Mr Justice Brian Walsh, Vincent Walsh, Zilma Walsh, Professor Trevor West and John Woods Senior.

My secretary, Joan Saunders, typed endless drafts and re-drafts and provided great encouragement at times when it was needed most and I thank her sincerely for her assistance in seeing it through to the end.

My wife, Marie-Christine, has had to live with this project and the disruption caused by having Arthur as a lodger in our home for many years and yet has retained her good humour and sanity throughout. In this, as in all things, she is my greatest support and friend. And then, of course, there is Ellen without whose loving attentions I probably could have finished this book in half the time and Eoin, whose arrival in February of this year was a great incentive to complete the task!

After much deliberation I chose to use Arthur's christian name in writing about my subject. I trust he, and those who knew him, will accept this as a mark of genuine affection rather than of undue familiarity on my part.

It is customary for authors to accept total responsibility for any errors in the text. While open-ended admissions of liability are anathema to lawyers, I gladly take all blame for any inaccuracy or other heinous defect.

I have dedicated this book to my mother. It is also dedicated to all of my family and to the partners and staff of Arthur Cox, Solicitors, who daily strive to uphold a glorious tradition.

Eugene McCague — September, 1994

1

Family Influences

ARTHUR Conor Joseph Cox was born in Dublin on 25 July 1891. He died in Zambia on 11 June 1965. He was born as the era of one colossus — Parnell — ended. He died as the era of another — Lemass — was drawing to a close.

In his lifetime, Arthur Cox was a brilliant student, an accomplished public speaker, one of the leading lawyers of his generation, President of the Incorporated Law Society in the centenary year of its Charter, a member of the Irish Senate, and a missionary priest.

Had he been born into any generation in Ireland other than that which at an early stage was destined to mould and create an independent Irish State, his life might have seemed even more remarkable. As it was, Arthur Cox's contribution to the foundation of the Irish State and to its growth into maturity, while not as all-consuming and self-sacrificing as some of his contemporaries, was none the less much more significant than a study of the public records of the times would have one believe.

If Kevin O'Higgins, Patrick Hogan, Patrick McGilligan and John A. Costello became more widely known than Arthur Cox, it was primarily because they laboured in a more conspicuous vineyard. He was friend, confidant and adviser to many of those who were in Government in the early days of the State. As his friend and colleague Terence de Vere White wrote in an obituary published in *The Irish Times* in June 1965: 'Nobody knew how many secrets were locked up inside that cautious head. He must have known the inner history of the early days of the State and of all its actors. Nobody has ever inspired, deservedly, greater trust. He was carrying a burden that must eventually have become intolerable but which it was almost impossible to lay down.'[1]

The private role which Arthur Cox chose as his contribution to the growth of the State mirrored the similar role in public affairs played by his father, Michael Cox, a generation earlier. Indeed, there are striking similarities between their two lives. Both were outstanding in their respective professions, Michael as a physician, Arthur as a lawyer. Both were confidants and advisers to the leaders of their generations: Michael to Dillon and Redmond; Arthur to O'Higgins, McGilligan and Costello. Both were Auditors of the Literary and Historical Society: Michael in 1872/73 in the Catholic University of Ireland; Arthur in 1912/13 in University College, Dublin. Both were Presidents of their professional bodies: Michael of the Royal College of Physicians; Arthur of the Incorporated Law Society. Both received honorary LL.D. degrees from the National University of Ireland: Michael in 1915, Arthur in 1952. Both were appointed to serve in public office: Michael to the Irish Privy Council in 1911; Arthur to Seanad Éireann in 1954. Both died in their seventy-fourth year.

In August 1961, shortly before he moved to Milltown Park to prepare for the priesthood, Arthur wrote the following note on his family's history to Ann Bodkin, daughter of his cousin Aileen:

> The Irish name of the great Cox was MacColidh. They changed to 'Cox' at the time of Poynings' Law, under which the native Irish were obliged to anglicise their names. Apparently this was done under some analogy between the sound of MacColidh to the Irish words meaning 'son of the cock'.

> They were the hereditary custodians of the 'termon' or shrine or relics of a St Barry. I know nothing of him, save that like Irish Saints of that time he used, when he had to make a voyage, to stand on the nearest stone and it would then convey him across the water. (I would refer you here to the amusing opening chapter of Anatole France's *Penguin Island* — except that it is on the Index and so one must not read it.) On one occasion, St Barry wanted to cross

the River Shannon in a hurry, so he stood on a stone and it took him across. My father had a little statue made of St Barry and the stone with him on it is now in the Church of Termonbarry on the Shannon.

The illustrious race of Cox centred in the Roscommon–Leitrim area now much depopulated. The name is still common there.

They cannot have guarded the termon very well because it has not been heard of for centuries.

Unfortunately, the shades have closed over their subsequent history. There was a Watty Cox who was pilloried before what is now the City Hall in Dublin but he was no relation. His offence was anti-Government painting.

One Kelly, I think the father of your great-great-grandmother, was a good duellist. I have a nice miniature of him and his two sisters. Each pistol is marked piously with a cross to show that it got its man.[2]

Michael Cox was born at Hillsgrove Lodge, Kilmore, Co. Roscommon on 20 September 1852, the son of Mr Hugh Cox and his wife Anne (née Kelly). He was educated at St Mel's College, Longford, and at the Catholic University School of Medicine. When John Henry Newman founded the Catholic University of Ireland in 1854 to cater for the children of Irish Catholics of the time, one of his priorities was to establish, as soon as possible, a medical school. In the summer of 1854 a suitable premises situated in Cecilia Street in Dublin (a narrow street between and parallel to Dame Street and Wellington Quay) was acquired and the Catholic University School of Medicine was formally opened in November 1855. F.O.C. Meenan in his history of the School describes vividly the struggle of Cecilia Street to survive against the backdrop of the social, economic and political upheaval of the late nineteenth and early twentieth centuries.

Michael Cox was a man of great ability and extraordinary energy. His colleague J.B. Magennis recorded that:

God had given him a fine stature, a stately figure, and a graceful brow. His physique was muscular; his fairish beard and moustache bounded lips full of firmness and strength; his eyes, deep-set, radiated sympathy with a latent power to threaten and command. His large face had the full temples denoting intellectual distinction and was almost ascetic in repose; but that countenance was constantly lighted up with the kindliness and gentleness of a noble nature, a generous heart and a versatile mind. He walked with assurance and humility; he listened with patience and forbearance; he spoke with conviction and understanding.[3]

He graduated from Cecilia Street in 1875. Initially he was a medical teacher. He later commenced private practice in Co. Sligo. In 1881, at the very young age of twenty-nine, he was appointed as physician to St Vincent's Hospital, thus starting a long and fruitful association with that hospital. He later became Senior Physician, a position he held at the time of his death. His appointment was the subject of some controversy but, as F.O.C. Meenan relates, 'Cox justified his appointment and became one of the most distinguished medical practitioners in the Country.'[4] He later became Consulting Physician to the Children's Hospital, Temple Street, to the Linden Convalescent Home and to Our Lady's Hospice.

Michael Cox's boyhood, spent in the depressing years following the Famine, had a profound influence on his career in later years. Although attracted to the life of a country gentleman, he chose to devote his great abilities to the service of the sick, particularly the poor — the principal constituency of the Sisters of Charity who ran St Vincent's. He was noted as a progressive thinker on medical issues and always adopted the most modern methods of clinical and laboratory research. His contribution to the development of St Vincent's Hospital was immense. In his last illness, when death seemed imminent, Arthur was instructed to amend his Will to include a bequest of £500 to the hospital 'as a token of affection and esteem'.[5]

Michael Cox returned from Sligo to Dublin in 1881 to take up his post in St Vincent's and established residence at 97 St Stephen's Green South. In 1886 he married Elizabeth (Lily) Nolan and they moved to 45 St Stephen's Green East. They had two sons: Aedan, born in 1887 and Arthur, born in 1891.

It is yet another illustration of how Arthur's life would mirror that of his father that 45 St Stephen's Green, in which the Cox family lived when Arthur was born, would later become one of the offices occupied by Arthur Cox & Co., Solicitors. Arthur moved the practice to nos 42 and 43 St Stephen's Green in 1926. The firm continues to practise from nos 41–45 to this day. The Cox family lived on St Stephen's Green until 1903, when they moved to 26 Merrion Square.

Despite the exacting claims of an extensive practice, Michael Cox was a man of very varied interests outside his purely professional work. He was involved in many philanthropic endeavours and had a keen interest in literature. In 1896 at the request of Lord Dunraven, the Chairman of the Irish Commission on Horse Breeding, he wrote a volume entitled *Notes on the History of the Irish Horse*. Prior to this, he had written another volume entitled *The Country and Kindred of Oliver Goldsmith*. He was a member of the Royal Irish Academy and a Fellow and Vice-President of the Royal Society of Antiquaries.

A generous proportion of his earnings was spent on books of every kind with an Irish interest. His library contained four fine sets of the *Annals of the Four Masters* along with many publications of the Gaelic League autographed by his friend, Douglas Hyde (*An Craoibhinn Aoibhinn*), and a good deal of Irish political biography. Michael Cox's love of books was shared by his son, Arthur, whose own collection would be extensive.

He was closely associated with the birth of the National University. He was a member of the Governing Body of University College, Dublin, a member of the Senate of the NUI and Chairman of its Convocation. A committed Irishman, he was an enthusiastic student of the language and frequently signed his name in Irish. He chose to attend the Catholic University School of Medicine rather than Trinity College or a college in England, a decision recognised by the newly formed National University which awarded him an Honorary LL.D. in 1915, to add to the honorary degree of M.D. received from the Royal University in 1895.

Having started practice in the West of Ireland in the turbulent days of the Land League, it was no surprise that a young educated Catholic like Michael Cox should have become interested in politics. The Home Rule movement in the early 1880s was predominantly middle-class — and upper middle-class at that. Michael Cox's elder brother Joseph, a much more fiery individual, became MP for East Clare and was imprisoned for his involvement in the agrarian unrest of the Plan of Campaign.

Michael Cox's first serious involvement with politics was while practising medicine in Sligo. He acted as joint election agent for the Irish Parliamentary Party for the constituency of Sligo in the General Election of 1880. He tried to persuade Parnell to stand in the constituency but Parnell declined the invitation, recommending in a telegram to Cox on 27 March 1880 that Tim Healy should be selected.[6] Healy, in turn, chose not to stand in Sligo. Instead he pressed on Cox the candidature of a young journalist and Parnell loyalist, Thomas Sexton.[7] Parnell then threw his weight behind Sexton, writing to Cox and his joint agent, a Fr McLaughlin, on 30 March:

Gentlemen,

My friend Mr Healy having expressed a desire that Mr Sexton's name should go forward for Sligo instead of his, I quite agree that no stronger candidate can be found — unless there is some local man of whom I have not heard — and I would strongly recommend Mr Sexton's claim to the elections. He has all his life been connected with the Irish cause.[8]

The election was a triumph for Parnell and his supporters. Sexton was elected in Sligo, with the help of a speech delivered by Parnell from the balcony of the Cox home. How different was the scene eleven years later on the occasion of a by-election in North Sligo, at the height of the leadership crisis, when Parnell again spoke in the county: 'Can you select the foul-mouthed Timothy Healy? Can you trust in uncertain and wobbling Tom Sexton ?'[9]

By now Michael Cox had moved to Dublin. He could count among his friends most of the leaders of the Irish Parliamentary Party. It was Cox who attended Michael Davitt at his death. After John Redmond had his motor accident, Cox travelled to Aughavannagh each night for several weeks to attend him, returning to Dublin in the morning to fulfil his hospital duties. Later, it was Cox who together with Magennis detected the intestinal tumour which was to end Redmond's career and life.

His closest friendship was with John Dillon, a friendship which began during his student days. They both graduated from Cecilia Street in 1875 and later walked the hospitals together. Dr Cox was viewed as one of Dillon's closest confidants and supporters. While practising in Sligo he risked his professional prospects by contributing to the effort, which was successful, to save Dillon from arrest. For a period, Cox was in almost daily contact with Dillon, acting as his eyes and ears in Dublin while Dillon attended Westminster. He was also friendly with Dillon's wife, Elizabeth. It was Michael Cox who attended Elizabeth Dillon when she died in 1907 at the age of forty-two.[10]

The singular facility not to divulge any matter told to him in confidence was a significant factor in the success of Arthur Cox as a lawyer and in his being entrusted with many tasks of great national importance. His father had a similar talent as is graphically illustrated by an intriguing meeting which occurred in August 1912. Among Dr Cox's more illustrious patients at the time was the Archbishop of Dublin, Dr Walsh. Concerned about his health, Dr Cox suggested that the Archbishop should take the waters at the wells at Marienbad, a fashionable spa in Austria and generously offered that he and Mrs Cox would arrange their annual holidays so that he could be at Marienbad at the same time.

Archbishop Walsh, his secretary, Monsignor Curran, and Dr and Mrs Cox were not the most distinguished pilgrims to the spa at that time. On one of the first days of his holiday, Dr Cox encountered another great ally of John Dillon, T.P. O'Connor, the MP for the Scotland Division in Liverpool. O'Connor had spent most of the previous week at Marienbad in the company of David Lloyd George who, in August 1912, was perceived as a true friend and champion of Irish Home Rule, his Liberal Party having introduced in the House of Commons the Third Home Rule Bill just four months earlier.

O'Connor, as Dr Cox would later reveal, looked 'the picture of despair' and with good reason, for Lloyd George, on the morning of his departure from Marienbad, had confided in him that he believed that part or all of Ulster would have to be excluded from Home Rule. There had been suggestions of such a course previously and a formal proposal by a Liberal backbencher, T.G. Agar-Roberts, in June of that year that four counties — Antrim, Armagh, Down and Londonderry — be excluded. That proposal was decisively defeated and, in 1912, even Edward Carson's muted support for partition was viewed as purely tactical, aimed at causing division in the Home Rule ranks in the hope that the entire scheme would be abandoned. The idea that such a senior Liberal Party figure as Lloyd George was tacitly accepting the need for partition was a major blow to T.P. O'Connor who recognised that any public revelation of this view would completely undermine the close relationship between the Liberals and the Irish Parliamentary Party and, in all likelihood, destroy the credibility of the latter and, with it, Home Rule itself. In his anguish, he shared with Dr Cox the entire contents of his discussion with Lloyd George. They agreed that they should not discuss the matter with anyone.

Monsignor Curran recalled Dr Cox looking preoccupied and not at all well on his return to the hotel that evening. Although he informed Archbishop Walsh and his secretary that Lloyd George had departed, Dr Cox said no more. It was not until two or three years later, when Liberal Party policy on the exclusion of part of Ulster from Home Rule was well known, that Dr Cox revealed that in August 1912, he had become, perhaps, only the second Irishman to learn of a British government plan to partition Ireland.[11]

In the New Year's Honours List of 1911 Michael Cox was appointed to the Irish Privy Council. This was a reward for his services to Lady Aberdeen, the wife of the Lord Lieutenant, in her crusade against tuberculosis in Ireland. It is a mark of the esteem in which he was held that he had the respect both of the Lord Lieutenant and of the leaders of the Home Rule movement. Disillusioned by the failure of the British Government to grant Home Rule to Ireland and outraged by the manner in which Ireland was treated in the aftermath of

1916, and particularly by the activities of the Black and Tans, Michael Cox resigned from the Privy Council, writing to the Lord Lieutenant on 2 September 1920 in the following terms:

> Your Excellency,
>
> Disapproving of the policy of the Government of Ireland, I feel it my duty to tender my resignation of the Office of Privy Councillor which I had the honour of receiving under happier circumstances.
>
> I have the honour to be,
> Your Excellency,
> Your Obedient Servant,
> Michael F. Cox.[12]

In 1922 he was elected President of the Royal College of Physicians in Ireland. In the following year he suffered a severe stroke. He was rarely seen in public after this illness, being effectively bedridden at the top of his Merrion Square home. His health continued to deteriorate and he was forced to resign from many of the posts, both professional and voluntary, which he held. In later years when Arthur referred to his father's illness it was always to speak fondly of that eminent physician as 'poor Father'.

While the continuing successes of his younger son were a source of pride and of solace to him, the tragedy of his elder son's life was a cause of great sorrow to Michael, to his wife and to Arthur. Following a glittering academic career in Belvedere College, University College and the King's Inns, Aedan Cox volunteered to fight in the Great War and served in the Royal Garrison Artillery. Like so many others, Aedan Cox went to war in an optimistic frame of mind. On the journey out, he sent his mother a postcard showing a picture of the R.M.S. *Munster*. The message read simply: 'We have had a very fine crossing and are just in sight of land. Hoping you are A1. Yours affectionately, Aedan.'[13]

The early innocence and enthusiasm was quickly shattered. Later letters to his mother describe, in harrowing detail, the conditions in the trenches. In 1917, Aedan suffered the loss of his left leg. His letters home sought no sympathy. Rather they were full of praise for the efforts made by the medical staff on his behalf. Though Aedan bore his suffering with great courage, he never fully recovered from the trauma of his ordeal. He returned to Ireland but, despite the love and support of his family, could not readjust to normal life in Merrion Square. He died, in tragic circumstances, in 1920. He was thirty-three years of age. The grief experienced by his parents was matched by that of Arthur who, throughout his lifetime, could rarely bring himself to speak of his brother's death.

Dr Michael Cox died, at home, on 20 February 1926. Tributes were paid to him by the many organisations and institutions he had helped in his outstanding career. Newspapers in Ireland and in England reported extensively on his death, recalling his kindness to his patients, his devotion to his faith and his loyalty to his country. Typical of the tributes was that paid by Surgeon McArdle on the opening of a new dispensary in St Vincent's on the night after his death:

> One other man is unfortunately unable to be with us to enjoy the vision of his hospital's progress. Through weary and often very trying times he was a wonderful counsellor, while in his medical work he was indefatigable; outside his professional effort he was the greatest example of thoughtfulness for the poor that has appeared in my long experience. So persistently kind, so constantly mindful of the trials and troubles of others, his mind must have been attuned by other than earthly influences. Need I put a name on the man who deserves well, not only of those he so generously relieved professionally, but of the people of Ireland, whose troubles were his troubles, and in whose success he gloried. This word picture is all too tame in depicting the life work of my colleague and life-long friend, Dr Michael Cox.[14]

The year of Arthur Cox's birth — 1891 — marked a significant watershed in Irish life. The previous decade had been one of frenetic political activity and upheaval. It had witnessed the growth of the Land League into a potent symbol of agrarian unrest, the formation of the Gaelic Athletic Association, the holding of the balance of power by the Irish

Parliamentary Party in Westminster, the conversion of Gladstone and his Liberal Party to the cause of Home Rule for Ireland, and the defeat of Gladstone's first Home Rule Bill. More than anything else, the 1880s had been the decade of Parnell. It was he who brought together the energy of the Land League's campaign with the wider aims of the Parliamentary Party; he who put Home Rule for Ireland at the top of the agenda of one of Britain's two principal political parties; he who, by leading a disciplined and organised political machine to the position of power-broker in Westminster, proved perhaps for the first time in her history that Ireland would be capable of self-government.

By 1891 the benefit of many of the gains made during the previous decade had been undone. The bitter split in the Parliamentary Party caused by the revelations surrounding Parnell's affair with Katharine O'Shea, the ultimatum delivered by Gladstone in response to those revelations, and Parnell's own stubborn refusal to resign as leader, dealt a cruel blow to the cause of Irish parliamentary politics. It would be nineteen years before the Parliamentary Party would again hold sway in Westminster.

In the week of Arthur's birth, his father's friend John Dillon, together with fellow Home Rule MP William O'Brien, was released from jail. On their release Dillon and O'Brien unequivocally denounced Parnell and sided with the anti-Parnellites — a severe blow to Parnellite morale which caused Tim Healy, by now Parnell's sworn enemy, to describe the decision as 'the greatest piece of news I have heard for ten years'.[15]

Three months after Arthur's birth, Charles Stewart Parnell died suddenly in Brighton. His death formally closed a turbulent chapter in Irish life. Professor Roy Foster has observed that 'there is a tendency to see the twenty-five years between Parnell's death in 1891 and the Easter rising of 1916 as a vacuum in politics: political "energy" being diverted mystically (and mechanically) into the channels of "culture".'[16]

The Parnell split indeed led for a time to disenchantment with formal politics. Literature became the new conduit for expressions of Irish nationalism. W.B. Yeats recorded that:

> The modern literature of Ireland, and indeed all that stir
> of thought which prepared for the Anglo-Irish War, began
> when Parnell fell from power in 1891. A disillusioned and
> embittered Ireland turned from parliamentary politics; an
> event was conceived; and the race began, as I think, to be
> troubled by that event's long gestation.[17]

The shift from political agitation to cultural revitalisation
provided the backdrop for Arthur's formative years. The
1890s, if not quite decadent, were a somewhat frivolous
decade for Dublin's middle class. Dr Cox abandoned politics
and concentrated on his practice, his writing and his love of
horses. The environment into which Arthur was born in 1891
was stimulating but very formal. His family was, by the
standards of Catholic families at the time, well-off. From his
father, he learned the virtues of hard work, of dedication, of
loyalty, of charity, and of patriotism. His mother was an
independent woman who ran the family home with great
care.

Number 26 stands on the north side of Merrion Square.
The houses are imposing three-storey over basement
Georgian town houses which were laid out in 1752 by John
Ensor for the Fitzwilliam Estate and were completed towards
the end of the eighteenth century. At the beginning of the
twentieth century they were occupied principally by
professionals, particularly by physicians. Dr Cox bought no.
26 from a Dr Yourell; it had once been the town house of Lord
de Vesci. Of the thirty-one houses on the north side of
Merrion Square which were occupied at the time, no fewer
than twenty-two were occupied by surgeons or doctors. Of the
neighbouring houses, no. 24 was the home of C.B. Ball,
Professor of Surgery at Trinity College, while W.G. Smith, an
ex-President of the Royal College of Physicians lived at no.
25.[18]

The Cox home was a sombre and gloomy residence. The
focal point was the large drawing room crammed with
paintings and furniture. The four members of the Cox family
shared this cluttered splendour with a small number of

servants and a variety of dogs and cats. Mrs Cox, in particular, loved dogs and throughout her life she was never without a canine companion, most of whom were christened 'Hedgehog' (or 'Hedgie' for short). The faded snapshots of the family which survive invariably include a dog. Arthur in later life had a passion for dogs, though he lacked any will to train them, and insisted on treating them on an entirely egalitarian basis!

Aedan, like so many older brothers, was Arthur's hero. There was great love but also rivalry between the two brothers, each vying for their parents' affection and approval. More adventurous, more flamboyant, more assertive than Arthur when they were children, Aedan was assumed to be the more brilliant of the two. This was partly due to the young Arthur's reluctance to speak. He did not utter his first word until he was nearly four years old, a situation which would cause concern to parents nowadays but which does not appear to have unduly worried the Cox parents. When he finally spoke, Arthur did not waste the momentous event on any childish attempt at either of his parents' names. Rather, as his mother indulged her passion for golf beside the North Dublin coast, Arthur startled the nanny looking after him by pointing out to sea and saying 'Lambay'. He would later claim to regret having broken his silence as thereafter he found himself obliged to reply to anyone who chose to address him!

Arthur's great joy as a child was to draw pictures of animals and of lakes and mountains. He was quite a talented artist. In later years, his interest in drawing was satisfied by constant doodling during meetings. The small bound books containing some of his earliest sketches were among the few mementos which he retained throughout his life.

The Cox parents enjoyed the outdoor life — Dr Cox with his love of horses, Mrs Cox with her enthusiam for golf. Dr Cox bred horses which he raced. His favourite was Blair Aedan which he brought for gallops over the Fifteen Acres in the Phoenix Park. While Aedan shared his parents' pleasure, being especially fond of hunting, the pasty and timorous Arthur was happier to remain indoors with his drawings and his books. None the less he participated enthusiastically in the energetic family holidays. They frequently went on cycling holidays in Donegal, the brothers maintaining a cycling register which recorded details of each stage and the distance travelled. Even at a very young age Arthur showed signs of developing the understated sense of humour which would become one of his trademarks, adding daily comments into the register, such as 'fritful (sic) road, very bad bends, won't go again'.[19]

2

Belvedere College 1900–1909

IN 1900, at the age of nine, Arthur went to Belvedere College. Aedan had started in Belvedere four years earlier. It is no surprise that the Cox parents should have chosen to have their sons educated by the Jesuits. To Catholic parents who wished to see their sons succeed in public examinations while at the same time receiving a broad education, the Jesuits offered the ideal programme of studies. Their stated aim of preparing students for the responsibility of one day being the leaders of an independent Irish State would no doubt have commended itself to one as patriotic and politically aware as Michael Cox. Belvedere College, the Jesuit flagship in Dublin, was a monument to the marriage of academic excellence and character formation which was the hallmark of its founders. Two years before the young Arthur Cox entered the school, James Joyce had left Belvedere for university and the world.

Belvedere College was founded in 1832. For its first nine years, the school (then known as St Francis Xavier's School) was located at Hardwicke Street. In 1841 the stately town house which had been built for Lord Belvedere — Belvedere House on Great Denmark Street — was acquired and 'the neighbourhood was treated to the unusual sight of Catholic boys going to school openly — unusual because Mr O'Connell's Emancipation Act was not so very old, and the former evil days were not far gone when Catholics must creep to their disguised academies furtively and fearfully, lest Dublin Castle lay its heavy hand upon their schools and on their masters.'[20]

The ethos of Belvedere, which was well-established in Arthur's time and survives in large measure today, can be traced to the arrival as Rector in 1883 of Fr Thomas Finlay SJ.

A supreme educator and independent thinker, Fr Finlay ensured that Belvedere was no mere stagnant Catholic version of an English Protestant public school. Indeed, it was not a 'public school' in that sense at all. Fr Finlay's philosophy of voluntarism and co-operation, together with his antipathy to the State — whether England or an independent Irish State — as the sole provider of moral values and economic support, ingrained in Belvedere's students a questioning outlook linked to a concern for those less well-off. As well as being prepared to govern in the future, Belvederians were taught to care for their fellow citizens through involvement in the social club established to help the poor of their own age who were forced to work as newsboys and the like.

Arthur's career in Belvedere from 1900 to 1909, was one of brilliant academic success. This success was matched by the emergence of a quiet competitiveness which served him so well throughout his life. While that famous school has produced pupils who are now more celebrated or renowned than Arthur Cox, it is doubtful whether Belvedere College has ever, before or since, had a pupil who so dominated life in the school during his time there. A note in *The Belvederian* — the excellent annual publication which recounts life in the school — for 30 October 1909, the day Arthur left Belvedere, says it all:

October 30

Before breaking up, we gathered in the quadrangle, and Father Rector in a short speech summed up Arthur Cox's brilliant career at Belvedere, and wished him the same success in the years that are to come. How we cheered our old companion and bore him round the quadrangle on our shoulders. But this was only a feeble attempt to express the esteem in which we held him. Then, to crown all, Father Rector said that next Tuesday is to be a holiday, to commemorate his great success. Bravo Arthur! Good-bye.[21]

The next entry in *The Belvederian* read simply: 'November 2. Arthur Cox Day. The Touring Club open the year with a visit to Inchicore.'[22]

It is unfortunate that *The Belvederian* was not published until 1906. We therefore have little information on Arthur's early academic progress, although it is safe to assume from his later record that he was always at or near the top of his class. His results from 1906 to 1909 were invariably second to none. The only student who offered him any serious competition was Gerald Delamer.

It was usual for each Grade to have examinations twice per year. At each stage Arthur achieved Honours and first place in most subjects. As is not uncommon with people who excel at subjects like English Literature, History, French and German, he had relative difficulty with Algebra and Geometry in which he rarely got Honours. For whatever reason, he achieved only a Pass in Latin in his Senior Grade examination although Latin had previously been one of his stronger subjects. This lapse did not prevent him taking first place in his class in Senior Grade.

The trend set in his Belvedere days of invariably taking first place was to continue for Arthur through his lifetime. Whether in examinations or elsewhere he had no interest in coming second. His academic brilliance was matched by a very competitive instinct. He was intensely proud of his pre-eminence as a student and later as a lawyer, of his record of coming first in examinations, debates or competitions and of being first to do or achieve a variety of things. For the moment, it is sufficient to skip forward to one incident which illustrates the point. Terence de Vere White told of how he wrote an article in *The Irish Times* in the 1950s in which he remarked that John A. Costello (then Ireland's Taoiseach) was beaten only once in a law exam. When de Vere White reached his office that morning, there was a message to call Mr Cox. When he did, Arthur, by now one of Ireland's top lawyers, said: 'I recognise your hand. You did not say who it was beat Costello.'[23]

In Belvedere, Arthur became involved in a wide range of extra-curricular pursuits. Sport did not feature among them. The many pages of *The Belvederian* dealing with cricket, rugby, athletics and a variety of other sports do not identify Arthur as having participated in any physical exercise. Indeed, there is no evidence of his having even attended any of the school's sporting events. He was a serious-minded and intellectual student. It is unlikely that his desire always to come first, which he usually achieved in intellectual contests, would have allowed him to participate in activities where his physical weakness would undoubtedly have led to mediocre results.

One pursuit at which he did excel was essay writing. The Belvedere Union — the school's very active Past Pupils' Union — offered a Union Prize each year for the best essay written by a student. The competition was generally seen as being for the 'big boys', but that did not deter Arthur who in 1905 became the first student from Junior Grade to win the prize. The title of his essay was 'Treasures of the Past'. It dealt with the significance to Ireland of its history: 'Her history is known to Ireland as her capital is to France, as her empire is to England, as her army is to Germany.' While his writing was not remarkable for one of his age it betrayed the self assurance which would be his hallmark in future years.

The fourteen-year-old Arthur was in no doubt that Home Rule would inevitably be achieved. The ending to his essay summed up the beliefs with which he was imbued both at home and at school:

> And so, Ireland cherishes them all, her history, her ruins, her memories. Robbed of her present, and uncertain, yet hopeful, as to what she may obtain in her future, she may ever find solace in her past. For even those pages of her history which are stained with blood and tears are witnesses to her undying conquests. She knows that all things come and pass away, and that the time will some day arrive when she may honour these, her treasures of the past, as they deserve. And then these 'treasures of the past' will awake to a new present.[24]

In the same year as Arthur won his first Union Prize, *The Belvederian* proudly reported that its past pupil, Aedan Cox, had been awarded the First Class Exhibition in First Arts in University College.[25]

In the following year, 1906, Arthur again won the Union Prize. His topic that year, more overtly political, was 'O'Connell's work for Catholic Emancipation in Ireland'. The language was more flowery. The sentiments reflected the growing mood of impatience which would cause young men of his own age to rebel within a few short years. Thus Ireland was portrayed as a nation which had suffered years of 'slavery, persecution and despair' at the hands of 'the oppressor'. His praise for O'Connell's achievements was without reservation. The essay, like his previous effort, ended confident that England 'will some day, be forced to atone' for the long list of wrongs done to Ireland. The final sentence of the essay summed up Arthur's view of O'Connell. It seems, in retrospect, not an entirely inappropriate epitaph for Arthur himself: 'And if it be a noble thing for a man to lay down his life for a friend, surely it is far more noble for him to devote it, till he sinks down exhausted, to the service of his people and to the honour of his God.'[26]

In 1907 he made it a hat trick of successes when he won the Union Prize for a third time with an essay entitled 'The attitude of England towards Irish Industries up to 1800'. The essay was altogether more weighty and substantial than his previous efforts and showed a maturity and understanding befitting a young man already showing signs of singular talent. The photograph which accompanied the essay in *The Belvederian* shows a handsome youth with a very strong cheek-bone and a very confident air who had clearly matured greatly over the previous two years.[27] The essay contained an impressive number of footnotes, evidence of the very detailed research he had undertaken to ensure that he would again be victorious in the competition.

It must have been disheartening, to say the least, for the other students to find Arthur winning the Union Prize year after year. Whether encouraged by his teachers or not, he voluntarily retired from the competition in 1908 to give other students an opportunity to win. *The Belvederian* described this as 'a generous action' which ought to arouse into action 'those who had feared to spend their time in unavailing effort'.[28]

While Arthur retired from essay competitions — at least temporarily — he quickly found a new pursuit in which he would prove equally successful and dominant over the coming years. Belvedere had been toying for some time with the idea of a College Debating Society. The driving force behind the initiative was Fr John Mary O'Connor SJ, affectionately known as 'Bloody Bill'. On 8 December 1908 the Belvedere College Debating Society held its first meeting. Arthur was appointed as its first Auditor. He would later be elected Auditor to every debating society he would join!

The topics addressed by the debating society in Belvedere in its first session reflected the many burning issues of the day and the willingness of the Jesuits to have them discussed. While there were the usual topics which might have been debated in any school at the time, such as 'That the Study of Modern Languages is more advantageous than that of Classical', there were other topics debated which were more controversial such as 'That Women should be admitted to the Franchise' and 'That Capital Punishment should be Abolished'; more political such as 'That the Irish Parliamentary Party is Deserving of the Support of Irishmen' and 'That a Republican Form of Government is more conducive to the Welfare of a State than is a Monarchical'; and more intriguing, such as 'That the Spread of Civilisation in the East is a Menace to the Security of Europe' and 'That a Surprise Invasion of England by Germany is not Possible'.[29] The records do not show on which side of the debates Arthur spoke, but for once he had to settle for second best when the medal for the best speaker of the year was awarded to his rival, Gerald Delamer.

It is the tradition in debating societies that the focal point of the year is the Inaugural Address delivered by the Auditor on a chosen subject and replied to by a number of invited guests. Arthur's choice of subject reflected his interest in Irish history and politics. His Inaugural Address delivered on 29 April 1909 was entitled 'A brief historical survey of the Irish Land question'. It was very topical coming as it did shortly after the publication of Birrell's Land Bill of 1909. His address finished in the same confident mood used to conclude his essays: 'At last the fate of Ireland is being placed in the hands of the Irish people, and it is now our duty to show that this confidence has not been misplaced, and that we are capable of taking our places by the side of a Denmark, a Norway, or a Holland as a self-sufficing and self-supporting country.'[30]

The guests invited to reply to his Inaugural Address included two controversial men of the time. Fr Thomas Finlay SJ, the distinguished former rector of Belvedere, was by this time the Professor of Moral Philosophy at the Catholic University. He also had a first-hand knowledge of agricultural co-operation on the Continent. He was a dedicated and vocal supporter of the co-operative movement and of its principal promoter, Sir Horace Plunkett. Supporters of Home Rule, like Dr Michael Cox, viewed the co-operative movement with grave suspicion as an attempt to kill Home Rule by kindness. They were particularly wary of Plunkett for his obdurate belief in the Unionist cause. Fr Finlay's speech was no doubt carefully analysed by Dr Cox who attended his son's Inaugural Meeting.

Dr Cox may also have had mixed feelings about the other distinguished guest speaker. Timothy Healy KC, MP was an outstanding advocate and a brilliant orator who, at the height of his powers, had held the House of Commons spellbound. His speaking talents were never more sharply or controversially witnessed than in his excoriation of Parnell in the aftermath of the O'Shea divorce trial. Healy was a political maverick who, at different times, enthusiastically supported and then vehemently denounced not only Parnell but Redmond and Dillon as well. He had rejoined the Parliamentary Party in 1908. He was later to become the first Governor-General of the new Irish Free State. It may be that Dr Cox persuaded Healy to lend his presence to his son's Inaugural Meeting, although the historian Owen Dudley Edwards has observed that the Jesuits were always anxious to be seen to maintain strong links with 'rebels' like Healy, perhaps even more so than with establishment figures such as Redmond or Dillon.[31] This radicalism may explain, in part, how the school produced revolutionaries such as Kevin Barry, Cathal Brugha and Joseph Mary Plunkett.

There is little doubt that the Jesuits paid special attention to Arthur during his time in Belvedere. The fact that his father was a distinguished physician, a close friend not only of John Dillon but also of Lord and Lady Aberdeen, and widely tipped to be a member of any Home Rule cabinet, may explain in part this special attention. It may also have been that the

Jesuits saw in Arthur a potential future recruit to the Society. He did consider going to Tullabeg to join the Jesuits but was dissuaded from doing so by his Jesuit confessor. The truth is probably more simple. In a school which prided itself on excellence, Arthur, regardless of his family background, deserved special attention because he was by far the most brilliant student of his time.

Apart from Jesuit teachers Belvedere had a large lay staff. Indeed by 1905, a majority of the staff were lay teachers. Of the many talented people who taught Arthur, the outstanding teacher was George Dempsey. Renowned as Joyce's English teacher, Dempsey in his near forty years at Belvedere became a legend. Arthur paid him this tribute on the occasion of his retirement in 1924:

> His genial smile and kindly manner invited friendship from the most reluctant and unwilling student; his strong character and firm will compelled respect; while his keen mind and lively interest in the wide range of subjects entrusted to his teaching awoke also in the dullest both interest and appreciation. Year after year examination results testified to his professional capacity; no less frequently his past pupils showed in some better way their affection and esteem. History, and particularly Irish history, he made a thing of life and actuality; literature ceased to be a question of books and broadened out to meet the confines of thought and experience; geography became converted from a dull affair of names and lists into what it really is, the science of all peoples and of the world. He was a great educator, and approached more nearly to the best ideal of the University professor than the mere school teacher; yet he surpassed the professor in this, that above all he taught character.[32]

The esteem in which Arthur was held in Belvedere by staff and students alike is amply recorded by the warmth and uniqueness of the celebrations which marked his departure from the school for the fresh pastures of the new University College. The photograph with his fellow students in their long coats and school caps milling around the steps in the school quadrangle is evidence of his popularity.

Arthur, for his part, enjoyed Belvedere. Its enlightened approach helped to nurture the introverted boy so that he left Belvedere a more confident and ambitious young man. He had found a forum where he could excel in his own quiet way, without constant comparison with Aedan. Indeed, he far surpassed his older brother's considerable achievements. He made many friends at Belvedere, some of whom remained close to him through university and beyond. Among these was one of his closest friends through life, not in the sense of intimacy or depth of feeling, but rather if friendship is measured in terms of continuity and loyalty.

George O'Brien arrived in Belvedere in 1908 to prepare for university. He had previously attended The Catholic University School and St George's College, Weybridge. Academically gifted, but socially awkward, O'Brien found it difficult to make friends at Belvedere. His backwardness at all forms of sport did not help his cause although, indirectly, it led him to find a soul-mate in Arthur, a conspicuous fellow non-game-player. The two revelled in each other's company, effecting interests in matters considerably more high-brow than their contemporaries. The story of Arthur Cox and George O'Brien is one of great friendship but also one of intense rivalry. By 1908, Arthur's position as Belvedere's cleverest student was unchallenged. The arrival of O'Brien represented the first possible test to that dominance. Since George started in the year behind Arthur, there was no risk of a head to head contest at Belvedere but that changed when both were in university.

As it turned out, Arthur and George O'Brien continued to avoid direct academic competition. It would be impossible — and unfair — to attempt, with hindsight, to decide what the result of such a contest might have been. Both were exceptional scholars but Arthur had one further attribute which might have swung a contest in his favour and which, indeed, was probably responsible for its avoidance: he was intensely ambitious, in contrast to George O'Brien who was altogether more timid. One result of this was that George tended to play a supporting role. He proposed Arthur for the Auditorship of the Literary and Historical Society in

University College, Dublin and was rewarded with a position on Arthur's committee.

When the time came for a direct clash in the academic field — they both proposed to sit for the LL.B. degree in 1913 — O'Brien withdrew at a late stage. While this was principally because he had his eyes on three other academic prizes that year — all of which he obtained — the news was gratefully received by Arthur who had earlier recorded in his diary that 'O'Brien and Costello are working like blazes!' On 22 May 1913 Arthur recorded: 'George O'Brien is not going up for the law exam!'[33] George's withdrawal allowed Arthur to claim first prize and avoided their friendship being put to a severe test.

After university, Arthur saw less of George O'Brien. The latter, in darker moments, would complain to friends that Arthur failed to keep in touch and failed to send him work during his short time at the Bar (O'Brien's career at the Bar lasted only three years before his health forced him to retire from practice). The reality was, as George O'Brien later acknowledged,[34] that Arthur's time was fully occupied by his busy practice, his many directorships and his responsibilities to his aged mother, his wife and his two step-daughters whereas George, in contrast, had short working hours, abundant leisure time and no dependants.

They did keep in contact at important times in their respective lives. When George was appointed Professor of National Economics in University College, Dublin, Arthur organised a party to celebrate the occasion. When Arthur was awarded an honorary LL.D. by the National University, George arranged a special lunch on the day of the conferring. George asked Arthur to nominate him when he decided to seek election to the Senate. Arthur ensured that while he was President of the Incorporated Law Society, George was invited to the official functions. Most noteworthy of all, when Arthur decided to marry Brigid O'Higgins, George was one of the first to be informed and acted as Arthur's best man. The importance they each attached to the friendship which had its roots in Belvedere and which survived their rivalry and their different chosen walks of life is summed up by James Meenan in his biography of George O'Brien, when he relates how pleased O'Brien was when Arthur, writing in 1955 in the Centenary History of the Literary and Historical Society, referred to O'Brien 'for whose lifetime friendship I am deeply grateful'.[35]

But back to Belvedere. George O'Brien succeeded Arthur Cox as Auditor of the Belvedere Debating Society for the session 1909/10. By now, Arthur had moved to University College. Following his success in Senior Grade, he won a First Class Scholarship in Modern Languages, thus creating a record as the only student who under the old Royal University of Ireland succeeded in winning a scholarship in the same year as he passed Senior Grade. Not content with this, he also won an Entrance Exhibition to the newly founded National University, becoming the only student ever to win scholarships to both the old and the new universities.

3

Life at University 1909–1913

ARTHUR Cox's career in University College, Dublin was from 1909 to 1913. It was a time of excitement and of change in the university and in Ireland as a whole. The Irish Universities Act of 1908 introduced by the Chief Secretary, Augustine Birrell, abolished the Royal University and replaced it with two new universities, Queen's University Belfast and the National University of Ireland, the latter having constituent colleges in Dublin, Cork and Galway.

A new initiative regarding Irish universities was, along with land reform, viewed by Birrell as an essential move if Irish Parliamentary Party support at Westminster was to be retained. Although non-denominational in theory the National University was intended and perceived as a gesture to Irish Catholicism. The process leading to the formation of the National University demanded that the Chief Secretary display considerable diplomatic skills in wooing the support of the Catholic hierarchy while not alienating the Protestant ascendancy and its loyalty to Trinity College and, at all times, retaining the vital support of Redmond, Dillon and the Parliamentary Party whose agenda was not necessarily identical to that of the Catholic Church. His refusal to appoint Fr Finlay to the Governing Body of the new university was, in particular, seen as a compromise demanded by Fr Finlay's detractors in the Parliamentary Party. The Party whole-heartedly supported the enterprise, John Dillon describing the Act as 'one of the greatest services to the Irish nation which it has ever been given to an English statesman to render'.[36]

The new college in Dublin opened in 1909 at 86 St Stephen's Green, replacing the Jesuit-run college which had

26

operated from the same premises for the previous twenty-five years. The first students to enter their names on the roll of the new university were Aubrey Gwynn (who later became a distinguished scholar and a Jesuit) and Arthur Cox.[37] Dr Michael Cox was offered the position of first President of University College, Dublin but declined.

If change was the order of the day in the university, it merely reflected the upheaval which was occurring outside. Arthur's four years in university witnessed the two General Elections of 1910 which left the Irish Parliamentary Party holding the balance of power; the introduction of the third Home Rule Bill and its rejection by the House of Lords; the formation of the Ulster Volunteers and the Irish Volunteers; the rise of Larkin, Connolly and the Labour movement and the Great Dublin Lock-Out in which another former Belvederian, William Martin Murphy, played an infamous role. A year after Arthur left college the Great War began to call young men to their fate. Two years later, in Ireland, all was changed utterly. Arthur himself, in recalling the period, would say:

> Had we but known it, the old world was passing away. Indeed, I recall about that time, when talking about the then Labour troubles, James Murnaghan, then Law Professor and since a Justice of the Supreme Court, said the time may come when you will look back to this as a 'Golden Age'. My period in the College and Society saw therefore many students who were destined to play a big part in the new Ireland, but many also who were fated to fall in the Great War or in our wars at home.[38]

The students who populated 86 St Stephen's Green in those exciting years were deeply conscious of the momentous times — the golden age — in which they lived. They were also quite assured of the prominent roles they themselves would play in the new Ireland. George O'Brien remarked that so certain were they of the approach of Home Rule that some neglected to prepare for a profession, believing that they would get a good job when self-government came.[39] The young Arthur Cox was even more confident, remarking to O'Brien that there were only three positions for which they were being fitted by their education: Prime Minister, Leader

of the Opposition and Speaker of the House of Commons.[40]
Each of those positions in an independent Dáil Éireann
would one day be occupied by one of his contemporaries.

The centre of student activity was the college debating
society, the Literary and Historical Society. The L & H had
been founded in 1855 shortly after Newman's college had
opened. From its early stages, it attracted the brightest and
best of the college's students who flocked to its meetings to
debate the burning issues of the day. Inevitably, in a Catholic
university, politics in general and self-government in
particular were rarely off the agenda. It boasted among its
auditors John Dillon (1874/75) and Tom Kettle (1898/99).
James Joyce was a defeated candidate in 1900.

By the time Arthur entered the new college in 1909, success
in the L & H was firmly established as a significant bench-mark
against which any ambitious student's career in university was
measured. It was natural, therefore, that Arthur joined the L
& H shortly after he entered college. What is more difficult
to explain is how, despite his shyness and his barely audible
manner of speaking, he became one of its stars within a
relatively short space of time. The answer lay in the
competitive and ambitious spirit which lurked beneath his
rather diffident exterior. What he lacked as a demagogue he
made up for by cultivating an individual style and humour
perfectly suited to his voice and to his physical frailties.

Arthur's involvement with the L & H had a profound effect
on his life in a number of ways. Firstly, the cut and thrust —
perhaps, more accurately, the rough and tumble — of the
weekly debates further sharpened his competitive instincts
while maturing him from the serious, overly academically-
minded youth who left Belvedere, into a more relaxed and
humorous individual. Secondly, he met, through the L & H
a number of people — particularly Kevin O'Higgins, Patrick
Hogan, Patrick McGilligan and John A. Costello — who would
loom large in the future governing of Ireland and would call
upon his talents in various ways.

The Minutes Books of the L & H for the period make rather
dull reading, simply recording who spoke at each meeting
and the marks (out of ten) awarded to them. Fortunately, the
Society's meetings were faithfully reported in the student

magazine of the time, *The National Student,* a publication in which Arthur's name was to appear frequently. Summing up his first year in the L & H, *The National Student* recorded:

> Mr Cox's maiden speech created a distinctly favourable impression. The matter of his subsequent speeches was invariably good, but his manner is rather irritating.[41]

In his second year in college (1910/11) Arthur became more involved in the L & H and more popular with its critical and demanding audiences. He was at the centre of the most exciting debate of that session which, for once, dealt with purely internal concerns. Women students were not entitled to become members of the L & H and several attempts to have them admitted had failed. On 10 December 1910 a resolution in favour of their admission was finally passed, but only after the defeat of a counter-motion to the effect that in the Rules of the Society the term 'members' should 'refer to male students only'. Arthur who had previously spoken against the admission of women, supported this counter-motion and, in league with John A. Costello, tried to have the meeting adjourned on every possible procedural ground including the well worn adjournment 'to consider the bad light'.[42]

It is doubtful whether Arthur felt particularly strongly on the subject of women members. He certainly had no difficulty in gaining support from them at a later stage. His stance was clearly tongue in cheek. His performance won him new friends including *The National Student* which reported that Mr Cox 'astonished all by a humour that formerly had been successfully concealed'.[43] It is worth noting that, in admitting women to membership, the L & H was the first of the influential debating societies to do so. Oxford and Cambridge would eventually follow suit but it would be another sixty years before women would be admitted to membership of the College Historical Society in Trinity College.

One week after the debate on women members, Arthur produced an outstanding performance on the much more mundane topic 'That Dickens as a Novelist is overrated'. By now he was a very popular speaker as evidenced by his topping the poll in the Committee election with 46 votes to 39 votes for his nearest rival John A. Costello. Later in the year he spoke on the question of the undue prominence of athletics in modern life and 'in a style of argument syllogistic and weird, drew deduction after deduction with such startling ease that not even a murmur greeted his discovery of an analogy between football and aeroplaning'.[44] He also proved himself adept at the annual impromptu debate where the speaker is given his subject only shortly before he is asked to speak. *The National Student* reported:

> Mr Cox emerged from the ordeal with flying colours, albeit one would never have supposed that his subject, 'That were it not for forgetfulness love would be unendurable', would have been so excellently handled by a gentleman of his ascetic demeanour. But still waters, as they say, run deep, and Mr Cox may have more things locked up in his innermost world than are dreamt of in our philosophy.[45]

Arthur's performances in his second year in the Society were good enough to win him the Silver Medal for Oratory, Patrick McGilligan winning the Gold. He also won the President's Essay Prize. While he had retained the academic slant of his earlier days, this was tempered by a quirky and off-beat humour which caused *The National Student* to say that 'his arguments, premises, minors, and majors are sometimes so positively weird as to lead one to doubt his seriousness.'[46]

Traditionally, students seeking the ultimate prize in the L & H — election as Auditor — seek election at the end of their third year as members of the Society. Arthur began the academic year 1911/12 determined to win that prize. The Society was in turmoil. The contest for Auditorship in the previous year had become so heated that the President of the College and the Solicitor General had been forced to intervene. Arthur dominated the L & H that year, winning the Gold Medal for Best Speaker. When the election was held, the candidates were Arthur Cox and John A. Costello. Arthur was proposed by his Belvedere friend, George O'Brien; Costello (a future Taoiseach) by Conor Maguire (a future Chief Justice). *The National Student* described the manner of Arthur's nomination:

Mr O'Brien rose to propose Mr Cox. He gave us a list of Mr Cox's successes from his earliest childhood up to the time he became a nut and went to dances. Nobody blames Mr Cox for winning a lot of medals — everyone must have his little hobby — but everyone blames Mr O'Brien for reminding us of them. Mr Davoren seconded, and in polished tones talked about the magnificent speeches which Mr Cox had made at every meeting of the Society. As Mr Davoren had been present at not more than three meetings this year his opinion on that subject was of undoubted value.[47]

Arthur appointed Martin Dalton as his election agent. Dalton proved an excellent choice, having learned much about politics from his father who had been an organiser of the Irish Parliamentary Party. The contest was keenly fought on both sides, but dragged on quietly, without much excitement. 'The only thing done by either candidate that could excite criticism was Mr Cox's action in collecting the votes of his supporters and keeping them until the last day for voting. We know that Mr Cox did this merely for reasons of convenience, but still it is not a nice thing to do.'[48]

He also cornered the votes of most of the women members with a campaign ploy which underlined the innocence of the times:

Everyone knows that it is the custom for the successful candidate for the Auditorship to invite (just a little stress on 'invite,' please) the members of the Society to tea after his election. This tea has for some years taken the shape of a smoking concert in the Café Cairo. The new Auditor pays for the tea, and as every schoolboy (emphasis on the word 'boy') knows, 'he who pays the piper calls the tune.' The lady members of the Society, thinking that they knew more about music than did Mr Cox, decided that he should pay the piper, and that they should call the tune. They, or at least some of them, held a meeting and decided to inform Mr Cox that if they did not receive invitations to his tea they would not vote for him. Mr Cox gave in, and 'bought their votes with penny buns'. That was the way some brutes of men put it.[49]

In the end, Arthur defeated John A. Costello by 112 votes to 63. It was by far the largest winning margin in an election in the Society up to that time. He became only the second person to follow in his father's footsteps as Auditor. Many years later, Costello reflected on the election and on his relationship with Arthur:

> My closest friend and rival in college was Arthur Cox. But compared to Cox I was the complete amateur. He knew every trick in the bag and always defeated me. At that time my only ambition was to become a back-bencher. Cox's was to get to the top of the legal profession and then become Prime Minister.[50]

George O'Brien remembered the election thus:

> If anybody had ventured to predict that one of the parties to this (1912) contest would have become prime minister of an Irish Republic his prophecy would have been received with some scepticism. If a hearer had chosen to believe that the prophecy would come true and had been asked to say which of the candidates was destined for this distinction, he would have unhesitatingly chosen Cox.[51]

Arthur's year as Auditor of the L & H was most successful and without controversy. Writing in the *Centenary History* of the L & H, he recalled two particular events from that year. The first was a trip to Manchester with Michael Davitt (son of the Land League founder) to debate on Home Rule. Those who argued for Home Rule lost the debate. To Arthur's deep disappointment, the detailed report of the proceedings carried in the following day's *Manchester Guardian* made no reference to his contribution!

The second was an event of national importance:

> At the great Home Rule Meeting held in 1912 in O'Connell Street, at which a vast crowd attended, filling the great thoroughfare from Parnell Square to Trinity College, the L & H was privileged to have a stand which backed on the O'Connell monument facing towards College Green. Michael Davitt, John Ronayne and I were among the speakers. This meeting was perhaps the highest point of

the Home Rule movement. It was not many months later that the split between the adherents of force and the Parliamentary Party occurred. For the moment, however, all Ireland, Redmond, Dillon, Devlin, and Pearse were united. At our platform the most dramatic incident was a denunciation by Ronayne of the Union Jack, which for some extraordinary reason had been hoisted over the offices of a newspaper at the Carlisle Building.[52]

The Home Rule rally took place in Dublin on 31 March 1912. Depending upon the sympathies of the writer, varying estimates of the attendance at 100,000 people to 300,000 people were reported. *The* (London) *Times* of the following day was definitely unimpressed. 'I do not think', wrote its Dublin correspondent, 'that the political effect of this demonstration will be very great. It was a good-humoured, pleasant, holiday gathering, simply proving that the Irish are a gregarious people and like excitement, especially on Sundays.'[53]

There were four platforms: Redmond was on the main platform, Dillon and the Mayor of Limerick on Platform 2, Devlin and the Mayor of Sligo on Platform 3. The fourth platform was occupied by professors and students of the National University, led by Dr Denis Coffey, President of UCD and Professor Swift McNeill MP. To have been on a platform on such an occasion was an extraordinary experience for Cox, still only twenty years old. The thought of Arthur addressing 100,000 people amazes those, who in later life, found it difficult at times to persuade him to speak to groups larger than two! It is interesting that the students who spoke at the rally were not among those of their contemporaries who would eventually play central roles in the creation of the new Ireland.

Arthur's time in the L & H was fondly summed up in a graceful compliment recorded in the *The National Student:*

Auditisne Arthur Cocem
Qui est nihil praeter vocem?

'To translate into plain prose, Mr Cox is possessed of such enchanting powers of speech that one thinks one is listening to some silver-tongued, disembodied spirit — an angelic Belial, shall we say?'[54] Arthur later said of this tongue in cheek compliment: 'I have always remembered it, because I am afraid it was true.'[55]

Arthur did not confine his talents in college to the L & H. He also founded (with George O'Brien) a new society called the Legal and Economics Society (later the UCD Law Society), which was largely composed of students of Law and of Politics. By the standards of the L & H its discussions were highbrow. As in Belvedere, both Cox and O'Brien became Auditors.

Arthur's extra-curricular involvements in college life did not detract from his studies. His academic career in university was as brilliantly successful as that in Belvedere. In 1912 he completed his Bachelor of Arts degree, gaining First Class Honours with First Place in English Language and Literature. By now the law was his chosen profession although, to the surprise of many of his contemporaries, he decided to qualify as a solicitor rather than follow his elder brother's path to the King's Inns. He would later say that his father had suggested that one son should become a barrister and the other a solicitor so that they could help each other. 'He never explained it would be all one way traffic,' Arthur liked to add.

Arthur's career choice required him to attend lectures in the Incorporated Law Society's headquarters, then located at the Four Courts. He was reluctant to sever his links with University College on receiving his primary degree in 1912. His position as Auditor of the L & H for the session 1912/13 required him to remain registered as a student in college. He therefore embarked upon two academic courses in 1913. He sat for the LL.B., a one-year law degree which was open to graduates of other disciplines but was not a prerequisite to joining the legal profession. He also researched an M.A. in English Literature, choosing as the subject for his thesis the Elizabethan dramatist, Philip Massinger.

He thoroughly enjoyed his last year in university. The position of L & H Auditor carries with it a unique status in college life, guaranteeing its holder a paramount position in student affairs and no small amount of adulation from those wishing to succeed him at some time in the future. His position in the L & H and his performance in his B.A. degree served to whet his almost insatiable appetite for further success. Far from resting on his laurels, the ambitious Arthur was determined that the year 1913 should witness further additions to his already impressive list of achievements. Doing well in the LL.B. examination, completing an M.A. thesis and starting work as a solicitor's apprentice would be sufficient to keep most people busy. But Arthur had found other mountains to climb. There were further scholarships to be won, more essay prizes to be captured, additional debating medals to be collected. There was a fourth debating society — the Solicitors Apprentices' Debating Society — in search of a new Auditor. He pursued all these goals with his usual tenacity. His diary for 1913 is a testament to his ambition and his determination. The inscription on the inside of his diary reveals his intellectual egotism which, for the most part, he kept very private but which strongly motivated him in his student days and, some would say, in later life. It read:

Arthur C.J. Cox, B.A.
Scholar RUI and UCD; Fr Delaney Scholar.
First Class Exhibitioner Arts and Law Schools.
Auditor L & H Society.
Auditor Solicitors Apprentices' Debating Society.
M.A.[56]

In his diary Arthur constantly reviewed his progress, admonishing himself for any minor failure along the way. Thus on the battle for the Auditorship of the Solicitors Apprentices' Debating Society, which he eventually won unopposed, he recorded almost daily details of the political machinations involved. On 7 February he wrote: 'Talking to Shaw. He will support me and thinks I will win in the solicitors.' On 12 February he noted: 'Binchy will support me for SADS.' By 15 February the campaign was going well: 'O'Connell says he will see that Morris does not get office. So that should mean me.' On 24 February: 'Prospects seem fairly bright.' By 19 May he could record: 'Shaw thinks I may get the SADS unopposed. Ryan tells me he hears I am going to get it. He stands me tea in the Café Cairo.' On 9 June, the wait was

over: 'Returned unopposed for the auditorship of SADS.
Thus is realised the chief ambition for 1912.' His entry for 9
April had listed his targets thus:

Present concerns:
1. Second Law in June.
2. M.A. (Massinger).
3. Auditorship SADS.
4. Coyne Scholarship.
5. Medal, Legal & Economic Society.
No news of the O'Connor essay.

By the end of the month, the news on the O'Connor essay
prize was good: 'Lunch with Davoren in Bewleys. He says
he will send in the O'Connor essays today. Apparently only
one other besides mine, and that is only three or four pages!
If that be so, there can be little doubt about the result.' On
1 May he reviewed overall progress:

As regards present ambitions, things at present appear
thus:
1. SADS Auditorship, fairly certain.
2. Medals, impossible to know but I have hopes,
   especially as regards impromptu.
3. L & E Medal, hopeful.
4. First Part LL.B., quite safe as far as getting through,
   O'Brien and Costello are formidable propositions.
5. M.A. probably alright, will have to work hard during
   summer.
6. Coyne, very little done.

Tabulated thus, the list certainly appears formidable. A
large part of the work is of course by now behind me,
whatever the result may be. The O'Connor essay is also
sub-judice, *res gesta* if not yet *res adjudicata*.

On 6 May, Arthur was awarded the O'Connor essay prize,
'the first score this year (except the inter-debates)'. His joy
was tempered by his concerns about the LL.B. 'God help the
second law! No work done! George O'Brien and Costello
working like blazes!' On 7 May he proudly recorded the fact
that O'Connor had written to Dr Cox saying that Arthur

would be 'one of the big men of the future' although Arthur himself carefully remarked that 'all prophets are not inspired!'

On 22 May the next of his goals was obtained, although his rivalry with O'Brien was such that he was not entirely happy with the result: 'Rather a disappointment in the L & E, O'Brien got the legal medal, and we tied with 9 for the Archbishop's Gold Medal for general debate. Thus, we exactly split the honours, I having got the essay prize.'

On 9 June, the Auditorship of SADS was his. On 28 June, in part thanks to George O'Brien's withdrawal from the LL.B. exam, Arthur could report: 'I am first in the exam — hurrah!' The runner-up, as he would many years later remind de Vere White, was John A. Costello.

On 4 November 1913 Arthur Cox was conferred with his M.A. degree. He obtained First Class Honours.

While Arthur's diary may seem like a chronicle of unbridled youthful ambition it was made more human by touches of amusing self-deprecation and by occasionally leaving aside his competitiveness. His entry for 27 April read:

> In looking over the part of this diary already written, it appears a very barren chronicle of events. I suppose it is the casual, that is for the moment, the most impressive. The name of mother, for instance, figures not much oftener than that of, say, Professor Kettle and yet I receive daily, hourly, kindnesses from the one and scarcely ever see the other! Such is my attempt at a diary! The important is omitted while the trivial is duly chronicled.

In addition to all his achievements, Arthur did enjoy more mundane pleasures: trips to the pictures with his cousin Aileen; teas at the Café Cairo (the fashionable Grafton Street student haunt of the time) with George O'Brien; walks in Dalkey with his friend, Ilene Mooney; excursions to Bundoran with his parents when on one occasion 'a marriage couple joined our carriage at Enniskillen, filling it with rice and confetti';[57] solemn ceremonies to mark deaths and anniversaries of assorted dogs — 'First anniversary of the death of poor old Tom. Peace be with him. He is buried in the garden';[58] dinners at University Hall in Hatch Street with

Jesuit acquaintances; concerts at Loreto Hall on Stephen's Green.

Arthur delighted in his name appearing in print (although he feigned to abhor it in later years). He was mentioned in Arthur Clery's book on the Town Tenants Act and reviewed for *The Evening Telegraph* a book entitled *Thomas Campion and the Art of English Poetry*. He was very pleased to be deemed worthy to share with Fr Finlay an entire footnote in an edition of *The Irish Monthly*, particularly — one suspects — when it recorded Arthur correcting the distinguished scholar. Fr George O'Neill SJ had delivered a paper entitled 'The Skylark and the Poets' which reviewed the role of the skylark in the poetry of Wordsworth, Shelley and others. The footnote recorded:

> In the discussion which followed the reading of this paper, the silence of Southern Europe as to the skylark, admitted as substantially a fact, was commented on — Reverend T.A. Finlay, SJ suggested that the explanation lay in the use by southern people of the lark as an article of diet and in the difficulty of treating what is used for food as a subject for poetry. This view, however, was countered by Mr Arthur Cox who pointed out that in Northern countries the lamb is beloved alike by the gourmand and by the poet.[59]

Above all else, he loved books. He was a voracious reader. In 1913 alone he delved into almost three hundred books, each faithfully recorded and numbered in his diary. His taste was catholic, embracing titles as diverse as Bram Stoker's *Dracula* ('not so terrifying after all'),[60] Maine's *Ancient Law,* Goethe's *Faust* and Shakespeare's *Twelfth Night* whose song 'What is Love, tis not Here After', Arthur remarked, had 'more genuine philosophy in it than in the whole of Wordsworth'.[61]

He was also caught up in the excitement of what was perceived as the certain coming of Home Rule. He recorded, with obvious delight, Liberal Party victories in Lithgaw and Keighly and bemoaned their defeat at Reading as a 'blow to Home Rule'. The date fixed for Home Rule was 31 May 1914 and each day Arthur recorded the number of days BHR (before Home Rule). On 15 July he noted the latest rejection of the Home Rule Bill by the House of Lords, but was not despondent: 'There is now a clear course before the Bill on its third passage. The House is no longer an obstacle. 319 days more.'[62] Arthur could not have had any inkling of the dramatic events which would unfold in Ireland and in Europe in 1914 and which would end any possibility of Home Rule being achieved.

It is not uncommon that promise shown as a student is not fulfilled in later life. Fulfilment of the ambitions of youth must frequently give way to more modest achievements. Many strive in vain to recapture the glory of their college days. But the 'class of 1913' was an exceptional one in extraordinary times. They were entitled to feel uniquely confident because they were uniquely placed to fashion a new Ireland. Externally, Arthur Cox was always the antithesis of the ambitious man, affecting a self-effacing manner and a distracted, ascetic character. The adjective 'eccentric' would, over time, become much more associated with him than would 'ambitious' or 'self-confident'. In many respects this suited a person who was under no illusion as to his own ability, determination and objectives. He was determined to bestride his newly chosen profession in the same quiet way that he had dominated his student days.

4

Birth of a New State

THE profession which Arthur Cox joined in 1915 was very different to that which he left in 1961. For one thing, there were no women members, women not being entitled to become members of the legal profession until the enactment of the Sex Disqualification (Removal) Act in 1919. The first woman solicitor in the Free State was admitted in 1923.[63]

The profession was affected by the First World War, not so much in terms of a reduction in business but by the loss of so many members who joined the war effort. The Incorporated Law Society strongly backed the war, the Council expressing its 'abhorrence and condemnation' of the 1916 Rising.[64] The economic position of solicitors remained relatively stable during the war but deteriorated in its immediate aftermath. The birth of the new State created new opportunities for work, especially for those like Arthur Cox who were on intimate terms with the State's founders.

To qualify as a solicitor it was — and still is — necessary to be apprenticed to a practising solicitor for a period of time. Arthur became apprenticed to Francis Joseph Scallan who with his brother John Louis Scallan, practised law at 25 Suffolk Street, Dublin 2. Arthur was related to the Scallans by marriage. Years later, as President of the Incorporated Law Society, he paid tribute to the Scallans and to Francis Crowley of that office whom he described as his 'teacher'.

The Scallans thought highly of Arthur. When he qualified in 1915 he remained with the firm as an assistant solicitor. When Francis Scallan died in 1918, John Scallan represented Arthur to be a partner in the firm. His name appeared on the notepaper of the firm and clients were circularised to the effect that he had become a partner. This was not in fact the

case and Arthur, who by this stage was very highly regarded
by the firm's clients, was not given any share of the firm's
profits.[65] John Louis Scallan died in 1920. In the same year,
Arthur, at the age of twenty-nine, decided to leave the practice
and establish his own firm. His decision was greatly influenced
by the suggestion that another assistant solicitor, more closely
related to the Scallans, would be offered partnership.

Arthur Cox & Co. commenced practice in 1920 at 5 St
Stephen's Green, a premises shared with J.S. Evans & Co. Ltd.,
Pharmacists. Arthur was joined by John McAreavey who had
qualified as a solicitor in 1912. McAreavey was originally from
Newry and had practised law at 23 Suffolk Street, two doors
up from Scallan's office. While the new firm bore the name
of Arthur Cox alone, John McAreavey and Arthur Cox were
equal partners in the firm until McAreavey's departure in
1930. The name chosen for receipt of telegrams was
'Litigation'.

The firm of Arthur Cox & Co. did not take long to establish
itself. A significant number of clients of his former firm, John
L. Scallan & Co., switched allegiance. Arthur was also quick
to make new contacts. One contact who proved to be a source
of considerable work for the new firm was Sir Horace
Plunkett. Plunkett had been Unionist MP for South Dublin
during the last decade of the nineteenth century. He was
more widely known as the promoter in Ireland of agricultural
co-operation. In 1894 he founded and became the first
President of the Irish Agricultural Organisation Society, the
precursor of the modern-day Irish Co-operative Organisation
Society. While by 1911 Plunkett regarded himself as a Home
Ruler, he was always treated with suspicion by supporters of
that cause. In 1923 his beautiful home at Kilteragh in Foxrock,
Co. Dublin was burned and a disillusioned Plunkett left
Ireland.

Arthur was introduced to Sir Horace Plunkett by George
O'Brien, who had met him through membership of the Arts
Club. O'Brien later worked in Plunkett House at 86 Merrion
Square for a variety of organisations with which Plunkett was
involved. O'Brien mentioned his friend Arthur Cox to
Plunkett and Plunkett immediately invited Arthur to
Kilteragh. James Meenan in his biography of O'Brien records:

'This was very awkward. Arthur's father was a close friend of John Dillon who had been a life-long opponent of Sir Horace and the co-operative movement. Arthur could visit Kilteragh only on condition of the strictest secrecy. Such were the smaller tensions of Irish life in those days.'[66]

Within a short time Arthur became friendly with Sir Horace Plunkett and later with the Secretary of the IAOS, Henry Kennedy (a brother-in-law of Patrick Hogan), whose daughter Helen became apprenticed in the firm. Arthur became solicitor to the IAOS and through this connection he came to advise a large number of the agricultural and dairy co-operatives throughout Ireland.

The principal sources of business for Arthur in the early days of his practice were those of his friends from college who were engaged in building the Irish Free State at the time when he was establishing his own law firm. While Arthur was intensely interested in politics, he eschewed any direct involvement in the momentous events of the time.

Given his early espousal of the Home Rule cause, and Aedan's involvement in the war, it is no surprise that Arthur did not approve of the 1916 Rising. He was acquainted with Joseph Mary Plunkett, a fellow former Belvederian, and in later years liked to recount the story of how he met Plunkett at a party in 1915. Arising from a discussion at the party, Plunkett began searching his pockets and pulled out a piece of paper which he looked at, remarking 'I suppose this is the only letter ever sent by the Imperial German HQ Army Staff to a representative of the Irish Volunteers.' With that, Plunkett, realising that he should not have such an incriminating document in his pocket, crushed it up and threw it on the fire.[67]

Dr Michael Cox remained loyal to the Parliamentary Party and vigorously opposed the rise of Sinn Féin in the aftermath of 1916 which saw that party win four crucial by-elections in 1917, a clear signal that the days of the Irish Parliamentary Party were numbered. He gave the United Irish League the use of his motor car for its campaign in the South Longford by-election in that year.[68]

The Parliamentary Party made an all-out effort to win the contest in South Longford. John Dillon personally directed operations and reported to Redmond: 'We have the Bishop, the great majority of the priests, and the mob — and four-fifths of the traders of Longford. And if in face of that we are beaten, I do not see how you can hope to hold the party in existence.'[69]

In the end, Sinn Féin was victorious by the narrowest of margins, only 37 votes. It dealt an ominous blow to the Parliamentary Party. This was followed shortly afterwards by defeat in East Clare, when Eamon de Valera achieved his first electoral triumph. The fate of the once-powerful Parliamentary Party was finally sealed in the 1918 General Election when it won only six seats against seventy-three for Sinn Féin.

Arthur supported the Treaty signed in December 1921. This was not surprising given that the Provisional Government, formed after the Dáil had ratified the Treaty, eventually included a number of his contemporaries from University College who were among his closest friends. Kevin O'Higgins became Minister for Home Affairs and Patrick Hogan Minister for Agriculture. Patrick McGilligan would join the Government of the Irish Free State as Minister for Industry and Commerce in 1924.

One of the effects of revolution is to catapult people of a very young age into positions of responsibility and leadership much earlier than would otherwise occur. In 1921, O'Higgins and Hogan were only thirty years old; McGilligan was barely thirty-two.

The burden of building an independent Ireland was exacerbated by the Civil War which broke out between the forces of the newly-established Free State and the 'Irregulars' — as the republicans who rejected the Treaty were termed by the Government. Another problem to be resolved was the uncertainty surrounding the precise effect of the Treaty and the status of Ireland as a dominion.

Arthur was involved in advising on certain aspects of the Treaty. The extent of his involvement is unclear. His innate discretion would not have permitted him to discuss it in any detail, although he did confide to a friend in later life that during the Treaty negotiations he travelled back and forward to London on the mailboat on eight occasions.[70] *The Irish*

Times in a profile of Arthur on the occasion of his nomination
to the Senate in 1954 recorded that 'He was ... one of the legal
advisers to the Irish delegation in Hans Place' and, for good
measure, went further and said that 'when the Provisional
Government was set up in Dublin, Griffith, Collins and the
rest relied largely on his advice.'[71] The Irish delegation which
took up residence at 22 Hans Place in London on 8 October
1921 included a host of expert advisers, as well as secretaries,
typists and cooks, but there is nothing in the detailed records
from Hans Place now located in the National Archives to
suggest that Arthur was ever in attendance.

There is a tendency to view the Treaty negotiations as
ending on 6 December 1921, when the Articles of Agreement
were signed. A broader definition would legitimately include
the further discussions which took place with the British
Government and with the Southern Unionists on the draft
Constitution which was finally published on 25 June 1922, the
eve of the elections to the new parliament.

The Constitution was primarily the work of the Constitution Committee established in January 1922, by the
Provisional Government shortly after it took power. The
nine-member Committee, nominally chaired by Michael
Collins, included a number of distinguished lawyers. By early
March the Committee had prepared three separate drafts for
consideration by the Government. The months March to June
1922 saw frenetic activity as Collins, Griffith, O'Higgins and
Kennedy sought to persuade the British Government that the
proposed constitution strengthened rather than abrogated
the Treaty.

It is likely that Arthur's involvement with the Treaty was
during the period when the Committee sat and the later
discussions took place. The single piece of formal evidence
of Arthur's involvement is an opinion on the Treaty given by
him which is to be found among the papers of Hugh Kennedy
in the Archives at UCD. Hugh Kennedy was the person
primarily entrusted with resolving the question of Ireland's
legal status in the aftermath of the Treaty. He was born in
Dublin in 1879. A graduate of UCD (it was he who had beaten
Joyce in the L & H election of 1900) he was called to the Bar
in 1903. He attended the Treaty negotiations in London as

legal adviser to the Provisional Government. In February 1922 he became Law Officer to the Provisional Government and was a member of the Constitution Committee.

It is worth pausing to consider some of the legal uncertainties which arose from the Treaty. The most fundamental of these was the legal status of the Treaty itself. The use of the word 'Treaty' implied an agreement reached between two sovereign States, but the de facto Government of Ireland which negotiated the Treaty had not yet established its legal authority over the territory it claimed to rule. The British negotiators were anxious to dismiss any significance in the choice of the term, Churchill believing that the word 'Treaty' was merely of 'great sentimental advantage',[72] while the Attorney General, Sir Gordon Hewart, defended the description on the simplistic basis that this was 'not an occasion for constitutional pedantry'.[73] Despite the dismissive attitude of the British, the relevance of the word 'Treaty' in the eyes of those Irish people who supported the Treaty was much more than symbolic. It represented an agreement between two constitutional equals, the Irish negotiators' status springing from the First Dáil of 1919. The status of the Treaty as an international, as opposed to an internal, settlement was an imperative to those who later promulgated the Constitution.

The second major legal doubt surrounded the nature of Ireland's future dominion status. De Valera in a private session during the Dáil debate on the Treaty demanded that it be renegotiated to reflect his own particular preference for External Association rather than dominion status, a distinction based on association with rather than membership of the Commonwealth and recognition of rather than allegiance to the Crown. Inexorably linked to this issue was the consequent legal character of the oath of allegiance.

While the Treaty threw up these and other niceties of legal interpretation, the reality was that the nature and effect of the Treaty was as much a political and emotional question as a legal one. Nonetheless, the Constitution Committee and particularly Hugh Kennedy were obliged to dissect its terms so that the draft Constitution could, as far as possible, avoid being attacked by the British as repugnant to the Treaty, or by de Valera and his followers as being even more repugnant to the Irish Republic than the Treaty.

Why, having regard to the quality of legal expertise appointed to the Committee, Kennedy felt it wise to seek an opinion from Arthur Cox, is unclear. The opinion is undated but its contents suggest that it was written in early 1922 after the Treaty debates and at an early stage in the Committee's deliberations. It is common for solicitors to seek the advice of Counsel on complex matters at law. It is rare that the roles are reversed. It may be that Kennedy merely wished to have his own views confirmed by someone whose independent opinion he knew would be respected. Kennedy would have known that if anyone's legal opinion was likely to be valued by O'Higgins *et al* it was that of the most talented of their contemporaries. Whatever the reason, it is a measure of the esteem in which Arthur — then only thirty years old — was held that Kennedy, who within one year would be Attorney General and within two Chief Justice, should ask his opinion on such an important matter.

The ten-page opinion delivered by Arthur to Kennedy was concisely argued and definite in its views. Its central thesis was that the Articles of Agreement of 6 December 1921 ended, once and for all, the right of Britain to legislate for Ireland and represented in fact 'nothing more or less than the Treaty of External Association for which President de Valera pleaded'. Arthur firmly rejected the contrary view:

> The opposition to the Treaty in Ireland, in so far as it is based on sound reasoning at all, proceeds apparently on the argument that the Treaty is not a Treaty of External Association but is a Treaty representing nothing more than an informal agreement between certain members of the British Cabinet and certain delegates from Ireland and accordingly that it does not constitute a firm foundation for the future independent (sic) of Ireland, or for the future good relations between Ireland and England.

He advised strongly that, the Provisional Government should make a firm stand with Britain on the issue and warned of the consequences of Britain being seen to continue to assert legislative powers in Ireland:

> It can readily be foreseen that any person in Ireland who chanced to be dissatisfied with any particular clause in the Constitution will at once seize on that as a handle to attack the entire fabric of the Treaty and that therefore the Provisional Government by acquiescing in any such course would be playing into the hands of its own critics.

He went on:

> While, at the same time, pointing out the possible benefits of a firm line being taken, on the other hand, it may reasonably be foreseen that if the Provisional Government takes a strong hand in the matter and insists once and for all on the British Government having no further power of interference in Ireland, that many of those who have hitherto doubted the Treaty will come to realise that in fact it achieves the object which they themselves have in view.

Later in the opinion Arthur put the consequences of further British interference in much stronger terms:

> Any claim by the British Parliament to legislate further for Ireland represents an encroachment of and an attack upon the liberties of Ireland and as such should be resisted to the utmost, even if (and this is scarcely to be expected) it should lead to a direct hitch with the British Government and a renewal of hostilities, because to give way upon this point would be to give way upon the whole.

He advised that the wisest course of action would be to convene a Constituent Assembly 'whose first Act would be to proclaim as the first article of the Constitution the principle that Irish sovereignty proceeds from the Irish people alone'.

The conclusion of his opinion is interesting in light of what was to occur: 'I would also point out that the Constitution of the Irish Free State having been created by the Irish Constituent Assembly, the words in the Oath contained in Aticle 4 "as by law established" could no longer offend any Irish conscience as the law would be an Irish one.'

By emphasising the sovereignty of the Irish people and the exclusive right of the new Irish parliament to legislate for those people, Arthur correctly identified the key elements in the Treaty on which its supporters could rely in extending its frontiers to meet the criticisms of de Valera and its other opponents while, at the same time, not unduly antagonising the British Government. The Provisional Government seized upon the fact that, uniquely among the dominions, Ireland's status arose from the signing of a Treaty. Their insistence on seeing it as a Treaty between co-equal sovereign States was given an international boost when, in 1924, despite serious objections from the British Government, the League of Nations registered the Treaty as an international agreement.

The legislative independence identified by Arthur as implicit in the Treaty further distinguished Ireland from the other dominions. Speaking in Dáil Éireann on 11 October 1922 Gavan Duffy, a signatory of the Treaty, asserted:

> We are not children of Mother England. When these various Dominions decided they wanted to become dominions they had to go to England for a British Act of Parliament, which was the very foundation of their authority ... We are not made Dominions (sic) by this Treaty, we are put in a status — we are accorded, if you like, the same status of Dominions, but we are not Dominions (sic).[74]

The Constitution Committee were imbued by the same independent spirit. The fruits of their labours represented a remarkable success for Kennedy and his fellow draughtsmen. The Constitution was the essence of a modern republican Constitution while, at the same time, it played sufficient lip-service to the theory of dominion status to receive British approval. Dr Leo Kohn wrote of it:

> It reduced to precise terms the conventional rules of the British Constitution. Its archaic symbols had to be introduced, but their meaninglessness for Ireland was writ large on every page. The monarchical forms paled into insignificance in the light of the formal enunciation and the consistent application of the principle of the

sovereignty of the people as the fundamental and the exclusive source of all political authority.[75]

The sovereignty of the people, which Arthur advised should appear as the first article in the Constitution, was enshrined in the Preamble, the Constitution being enacted on the authority which came 'from God to the people'. Article 1 declared Ireland to be a co-equal member of the Commonwealth while Article 2 declared: 'All powers of government and all authority legislative, executive, and judicial in Ireland, are derived from the people of Ireland.'

Unfortunately, the request from Kennedy to Arthur for his opinion and any reactions to it have not survived. It is impossible therefore to assess what importance, if any, was attached to it. The fact that virtually every one of its recommendations was ultimately followed is, at the very least, a tribute to Arthur's prescience. The Dáil, sitting as a Constituent Assembly, duly enacted the Constitution of the Irish Free State, the relevant Bill having been conducted through its various stages with remarkable skill by Kevin O'Higgins. It was only in relation to attitudes to the oath that Arthur's opinion would prove invalid.

The General Election held in June 1922 represented a significant victory for the supporters of the Treaty. The Third Dáil assembled on 9 September 1922 and the new Government set about the task of creating the framework for a new State. Central to its plans was the long-term goal of a coherent industrial development policy. To a great extent this was overshadowed by the short-term imperative of ensuring the security and very survival of the new State. Arthur would be, in time, inextricably linked with the achievement of the long-term industrial goal. For a time he apparently found himself involved also in the murky end of the State's existence.

It has been suggested that in late 1922 and early 1923 Arthur allowed his office bank account to be used as a means of making secret payments to an organisation known as the Citizens' Defence Force. Very little is known of the activities of the CDF and, consequently, of any involvement Arthur may have had with it.

The shift from armed revolution to constitutional democracy is one which in every fledgling State is fraught with difficulty. The Irish experience was particularly traumatic given the viciousness of the Treaty split and the death, on the pro-Treaty side, of Michael Collins. The new Government had to face not only the increasing hostility of the anti-Treaty Irregulars but the uncertain loyalty of sections of the army. Paranoia about the enemy within was as compelling as fear of the enemy without.

Central to this problem was the role of the Irish Republican Brotherhood. Though in the early days of the Civil War it was assumed by many including O'Higgins to be extinct, it continued to exist as a rallying point for those in the army and elsewhere who distrusted the manner in which the Treaty was becoming institutionalised and who believed that Collins's view of the Treaty as merely a stepping stone to a fully independent Ireland with no formal links to Britain was being conveniently ignored. The IRB was, in O'Higgins's words, 'galvanised into life' in early 1923 when a number of influential army officers, led by Major General Liam Tobin and Charles F. Dalton established an army within an army in the form of the Irish Republican Army Organisation. The tensions caused by this move would lead to open mutiny at the Curragh Camp in 1924 and would be largely responsible for the resignation of two Government ministers.

It is against this background, as well as the more obvious one of the Civil War, that the growth of organisations like the CDF must be viewed. The Government's obsession with security led to the creation of three separate secret service groups. The most prominent of these was the Criminal Investigation Division which operated from Oriel House in Westland Row. Its function was to investigate and interrogate suspected members or supporters of the Irregulars. Its seventy-five officers gained a reputation for ruthlessness and, at times, for savagery. Oriel House became a potent symbol of fear for the Irregulars. While the form of interrogation may not have justified the belief that 'the terrors of the Spanish Inquisition were mere lullabies to the treatment meted out to prisoners by the officers of the CID',[76] it was not so refined as to merit the description of 'judicious' given to it by one of its proponents.

The second group was the Protective Officers Corps whose function was to protect the houses and persons of Ministers, Deputies, Senators and Government officials, including Ministers McGrath and O'Higgins, Senators Lord Glenavy, Yeats and Gogarty as well as Hugh Kennedy and Gordon Campbell. At its height it comprised 170 men.

The Citizens' Defence Force was the final weapon in the State security armoury. It consisted of 100 officers and men on full-time duty and fifty part-time volunteers. Its functions were to protect Oriel House (and later 88 Merrion Square to which premises the CID moved) and city cinema theatres as well as collecting intelligence on Irregular activities.[77]

The CDF differed from the CID and the Protective Officers Corps in a number of important respects. While both of the other organisations were under the control of Capt. P.M. Moynihan and were answerable to Oriel House, the CDF was supervised by Capt. Henry Harrison who reported to Dublin Castle.

Harrison was an extraordinary figure. Born in England, his first visit to Ireland was as a student from Balliol College, Oxford, who travelled with his tutor to witness evictions in Gweedore. Outraged by what he saw, he became embroiled in a fracas with the police which brought him to the attention not only of the authorities but of Parnell who persuaded him to join the Parliamentary Party. In 1890, at the age of twenty-three and still a student, he became MP for mid-Tipperary. He sided unswervingly with Parnell throughout the split and remained loyal to him to the end. In 1912 he became Secretary of the Stephen's Green Club, a position he vacated in 1916 to join the Royal Irish Regiment in France. Wounded in action and awarded the MC and the OBE, he returned to Ireland, worked with the Irish Dominion League and enthusiastically supported the Treaty. He later wrote a number of political pamphlets and books including *Parnell Vindicated,* a powerful retrospective on his leader and hero.

Harrison was persuaded to form the CDF following an approach from Kevin O'Higgins. In contrast to the CID, the activities of the CDF were uncontroversial. There is no evidence to suggest that in its few months of existence it was involved in anything more sinister than gathering intelligence at a fairly low level. The other distinguishing feature of the CDF was that it was financed through a separate secret service vote.

The Estimate approved by the Government for all secret service activities (at that stage, mainly the CID) for the year ended 31 March 1923 was the sum of £220,000, testament in itself to how seriously the Government viewed the threat to the security of the State.[78] As it happened, an amount of £127,000 was actually spent. For the year to 31 March 1924 the smaller sum of £47,574 was set aside for the CID and Protective Officer Corps.[79] The separate expenditure of the CDF was, by contrast, only £6,050.[80]

The fact that the CDF formed part of a security system aimed at protecting the fabric of the new State being built by a number of his closest friends would have made it virtually impossible for Arthur to refuse to assist, although — in common with so many other things that may or may not have occurred during the Civil War — evidence in support of his involvement is no more than a mixture of hearsay and folklore.

The CDF did not exist for very long. In October 1923, despite opposition from Joseph McGrath, O'Higgins persuaded the Cabinet to disband all three secret service organizations. The ending of the Civil War required their dismantling so that more conventional army and police forces could be established.

The development of an industrial policy was likewise a daunting task. None of the new Cabinet could claim any significant expertise in financial or economic planning. O'Higgins, Hogan and McGilligan had studied economics at UCD but this in itself did not qualify them to formulate structures for an economically fragile fledgling State. The one Irish political leader who had a clearly defined view of economic policy was Arthur Griffith, but he had died in August of that year.

The lack of experience in the Cabinet was exacerbated by the conservatism of the civil service which, by and large, consisted of the same men who had been in charge prior to the Treaty. They retained the values which had underpinned British policy in Ireland but which were not necessarily suitable for a new independent State: financial stringency coupled with a strong aversion to State intervention as a part of industrial policy. Kevin O'Higgins proclaimed himself proud of the fact that he and his colleagues were 'probably the most conservative minded revolutionaries that ever put through a successful revolution'.[81] By contrast, a disillusioned McGrath described the position in 1924 as 'government by a clique and officialdom of the old regime'.

The new State eventually gave birth to a new elite. As with the civil service, the old establishment continued to hold significant sway but the influence of the Catholic professional classes grew steadily throughout the 1920s. Perhaps no individual, outside the Cabinet, benefitted more from this shift than Arthur Cox. His influence, direct and indirect, on the shaping of industrial policy over the next three decades was immense. His advice was eagerly sought not alone by State agencies but also by industrialists, both domestic and foreign, wishing to deal with or find ways around the regulations which governed those same agencies. The inevitable result of this was that despite his scholarship, his love of languages and drama and his ascetic demeanour, Arthur became essentially a man of business. His firm's client list was, from its earliest days, made up in large measure of corporate clients. It was in the field of company law that he achieved most prominence. His breadth of knowledge of other areas of law and of life was of great assistance in advising businessmen on their problems. A 1958 profile in *The Irish Times* expressed it thus:

> ... there are times when people realise the value of an experienced adviser who is prepared to listen to their troubles, to warn, and to recommend. If to experience of the world and natural capacity can be added scholarship and wide reading, such an adviser is invaluable, because he

will see problems in better perspective than one who has pursued a narrow way with strictly limited object. Very few lawyers in any time, in any country, brought to their work a mind so richly cultivated as that of Arthur Cox.[82]

Arthur was closely involved in advising on the single most ambitious project of the new Government, the national electrification scheme leading to the establishment of the Electricity Supply Board. In their history of the ESB, Maurice Manning and Moore McDowell suggest that the electrification scheme

> offered almost at once a possible basis for industrial development and agricultural improvement; equally importantly, it could be seen as an act of faith by the Government in the future of the State, something which was urgently required after the psychological demoralisation of the Civil War. It was important for the Government that it should do something major and dramatic, and it is clear that, after some initial caution, the Executive Council hit upon the idea of a national electrification scheme as fitting this description.[83]

Arthur's involvement with the scheme was not as a result of a request for advice from the Government. Rather, the initial approach came from the man who is generally credited with having sold the Shannon Scheme to the Government. Dr T.A. McLaughlin entered University College, Dublin in 1914, the year after Arthur graduated. Having taken a degree in mathematics and physics, he went to University College Galway where in 1922 he took a degree in electrical engineering. In December of that year Dr McLaughlin was offered and accepted a job with Siemens Schuckert in Berlin. There he acquainted himself with the manufacture of all kinds of electrical machinery and with the transmission and distribution of electricity.

Dr McLaughlin became convinced that water-generated electricity was essential for Ireland's development. He quickly persuaded his German employers that they should authorise him to open discussions with the Irish Government with a view to Siemens Schuckert providing the expertise for the

construction of a hydroelectric scheme on the River
Shannon. In November 1923 Dr McLaughlin contacted
Patrick McGilligan whom he had known in UCD, and
McGilligan in turn introduced him to W.T. Cosgrave. By
February 1924 the Department of Industry and Commerce
had issued a letter to Siemens outlining the basis on which
the Government would proceed. The appointment of
McGilligan as Minister for Industry and Commerce in April
1924 served to fuel the enthusiasm in Government for the
project. In August 1927 the Electricity Supply Board was
established and in October 1929 the Shannon hydroelectric
scheme commenced operation.

As well as making contact with Patrick McGilligan, Dr
McLaughlin also sought the assistance of Arthur Cox who
became solicitor to Siemens Schuckert and advised the
company on its negotiations with the Government. Whether
Dr McLaughlin was encouraged by McGilligan to retain
Arthur's services is unclear — his mother had been a patient
of Dr Cox and this may have been the connection. At any rate,
within a short space of time, Arthur Cox and Dr Tommy
McLaughlin struck up a very close working relationship. They
also became good friends. Together they formed a National
University Graduates' Association which C.S. (Todd)
Andrews would later describe as 'a non-political organisation'
with 'a useful secondary effect of at least permitting polite
conversation between Republicans and Free Staters'.[84]

There began a connection between Arthur Cox & Co. and
the McLaughlin family which proved extremely fruitful and
survives to this day. In 1927 Dr Tommy McLaughlin's younger
brother Niall became apprenticed to Arthur. He later became
a partner in the firm, retiring as senior partner in the 1980s.
He remains a consultant to the firm. The links continue
through Niall's sons, Paul and Peter, who are now partners in
the practice.

It is not surprising that Arthur Cox and Dr Tommy
McLaughlin got on well together. McLaughlin, like Arthur,
was self-confident and ambitious. A description of his time at
Synge Street CBS is remarkably similar to descriptions of
Arthur at Belvedere: 'The folk memory of McLaughlin
amongst Synge Street boys was of being indifferent to any of
the usual schoolboy interest in games. He concentrated on

his lessons with great success. Any exhibitions, scholarships or prizes that were available he won.'[85]

It was clearly of assistance to Siemens to have on their side someone as formidable and as well-connected as Arthur. He had no difficulty in making use of his personal contacts with his old friend Patrick McGilligan as Minister for Industry and Commerce. When a dispute arose in respect of payments to be made to Siemens under its contract with the Government he wrote to McGilligan at his home, addressing the Minister by the name used only among his intimates: 'Dear Tody, sometime that you are free would you please give me a ring as I would like to have a further word with you about the SSL matter.'[86] It was also of no little help that Arthur — to the amazement of the Siemens representatives and particularly of Frederick Weckler who would later join the Board of the ESB — conducted their meetings in German! Years later, German investors in Roscrea Meat Products who conducted a discussion in their native tongue on the assumption that the Irish advisers present would not understand them were deeply embarassed when Arthur once more displayed his linguistic talents on showing them to the door!

Arthur's work for Siemens, the knowledge of the electricity business he gained from it, and his friendship with Tommy McLaughlin and with Patrick McGilligan combined to make him the obvious choice as Law Agent to the ESB on its formation in 1927, a position he held for the remainder of his legal career. The ESB was a significant source of work to Arthur who, in turn, ensured that this essential national resource had available to it at all times the benefit of his legal knowledge and his commercial good sense.

Over the years Arthur became particularly friendly with the Chairman of the ESB, Richard Browne. Dick Browne (or 'Electricity Browne' as he was known to many in Dublin) had been an Income Tax Inspector. He was friendly with John A. Costello (then Attorney General) and was nominated by the Government as Chairman of the ESB in 1930.

Dick Browne and Arthur Cox could not have been more different. Browne was a distinguished looking man, tall and elegant, with ruddy features and a magnificent crop of thick white hair. He was a stylish dresser who had his suits made by a London tailor, rarely wearing the same suit on consecutive days. He was interested in ballroom dancing, antique furniture and classical music. He was fond of dining in good restaurants and, for a time, was President of the Dublin Food and Wine Society. By contrast, Arthur was almost totally ascetic, rarely eating, never drinking and renowned for his lack of dress sense.

Yet the two were friends for over thirty years, meeting nearly every week for lunch, which in Arthur's case usually consisted of coffee and a bun. A solemn ritual was observed whereby Browne would telephone Arthur to check if he was available and if they would meet. Arthur would mumble 'yes' to each question and no further chat would ensue. They were a strange sight as they wandered along St Stephen's Green together, few words passing between them. On more than one occasion Dick Browne was the subject of praise from passers-by for being so charitable as to take to lunch a man who was so evidently — from his appearance — down on his luck!

A measure of the trust placed in Arthur in the early days of the State can be gleaned from the reports of the proceedings in Dáil Éireann for 15 March 1927. On that day, the Minister for Industry and Commerce, Patrick McGilligan, introduced the Second Reading of the Electricity Supply Bill with which Arthur was closely involved. Immediately prior to this, the Minister for Lands and Agriculture, Patrick Hogan, had made a major statement on the policy of the Government for the reorganisation and development of the Irish dairy industry when introducing a Supplementary Estimate for his Department.

The Supplementary Estimate was required to facilitate the funding by the Government of the purchase of the Condensed Milk Company of Ireland. The company was a very large concern owning in Ireland 113 creameries, ten condensed milk plants and other assets including a toffee factory bought earlier from the liquidator of Cleeves Ltd. Its principal shareholders were Messrs Lovell and Christmas of London. The company had been in fierce competition with the Irish co-operatives for milk supplies. This trade war led to Government concern that banks would seek repayment of loans due by a number of co-operatives which, in turn, would lead to a crisis in the dairy industry as a whole. The company, for its part, did not relish a prolonged price war. In the end, it was decided that the company should be acquired and that the Government should intervene and fund the purchase.

The Government's decision to intervene in such a direct manner in private enterprise flew in the face of the non-interventionist stance adopted up to then. Patrick Hogan rationalised this *volte-face* on the basis of the central role of agriculture in the economy. He defended the policy against claims that it would establish a monopoly — 'I admit it — a most unusual monopoly: a monopoly of all the producers' — and that it would shelter the dairy industry from competition, 'It is rather an attempt to enable the industry to meet the organised competition of Denmark, New Zealand, Australia and Canada. This competition is quite sufficient to go on with and to keep the industry on its mettle.'[87]

The negotiation of the deal to purchase the Condensed Milk Company was conducted by Arthur in his capacity as solicitor to the IAOS. Arthur was almost solely responsible for agreeing the price of £365,000. The Government was happy to rely entirely on him to agree the deal and the Supplementary Estimate voted through in March 1927 was to allow Arthur to complete the purchase. The funding of the acquisition of the Condensed Milk Company was a major step by the Government which saw it as essential to the development of the dairy industry, just as the Shannon Scheme was essential to the development of industry in general.

Despite his close friendship with many Ministers in the Government, Arthur was not tempted to seek election to public office. When graduating from University College, Dublin with Home Rule seeming imminent, attempts were made to persuade him to commence practice in Kerry with a view to standing as a member for that county in the expected new Irish Parliament. Later, he came under pressure from his friends to seek elected office. Kevin O'Higgins, in particular, was anxious to see Arthur's talents being put to use in a direct manner in political life. The General Election of 1927 had the added challenge to the Government of the new political party founded by de Valera in the previous year — Fianna Fáil. It was essential that the Government field the strongest possible list of candidates. To this end, O'Higgins wrote to Arthur on 21 April 1927. Having acknowledged a donation of £100 (a considerable sum at the time) and having assured Arthur that anonymity would be secure, O'Higgins went on:

> J McG has not decided to stand. It would be overstating the position to say that he has decided not to stand. The last I have from that quarter is that he would not stand if he had an assurance that the Government would be at pains to secure him a seat in the Senate. I am all in favour of giving him that assurance. I could think of many people who would be much more ornamental on the river's brim and much more soothing to the desert air than you. Your existence needs other justification.[88]

We can only assume that Arthur gave his friend's exhortations careful consideration before declining the invitation. It would have been difficult for him to give up his law practice, even temporarily, having regard to the reputation he had already built up. More significantly, the election of June 1927 came just over one year after his father's death. With Aedan and his father both gone, Arthur was responsible for the welfare of his mother with whom he still lived in Merrion Square. His natural shyness made him an unlikely candidate for the hustings. Whatever the reason, Arthur chose not to seek election. Cosgrave's party was returned with the largest number of seats. In the new Government, O'Higgins was Vice-President of the Executive Council, Minister for Justice and Minister for External Affairs.

On 10 July 1927 Kevin O'Higgins was shot on his way to Mass in Booterstown, Co. Dublin. He was brought back to his home where he lingered in dreadful agony but in unquenched spirit for over five hours as friends and colleagues came to say their goodbyes. Arthur was one of those who visited this harrowing scene. Kevin O'Higgins was thirty-five years of age when he died. His death deprived Ireland of a most controversial figure of undoubted courage. Arthur was devastated by O'Higgins's death. He viewed O'Higgins as the outstanding figure of an extraordinary generation. He later wrote of him:

> His will was inflexible, his courage as shown by his death as by his life, was unshakeable. He had above all a deeply

rooted sense of justice — that quality which Aristotle first
and all after him have seen to be the keystone of every
justifiable state. He had a clear and lucid intelligence. He
had the calm of a seaman in a great gale. He deserves
to rank amongst the greatest of state builders, building for
the true destiny of his people. Other men had greater
colour, greater appeal, but he was strength. And his
strength held the reins until the course was won and
Ireland for the first time had a firm government of her own
people, for her own people.[89]

In the immediate aftermath of O'Higgins's assassination,
pressure was again exerted on Arthur to seek election. On 18
July, eight days after O'Higgins's death, Arthur received a
poignant note from O'Higgins's widow:

Dear Mr Arthur Cox,

I cannot allow this time to pass without telling you what
your dead friend, darling Kevin thought of you. 'There are
two men whose opinion I would always seek in any crisis
and whose judgement I believe I would accept with
gratitude, Arthur Cox and James Hogan.' He was most
anxious that you should be elected at the last elections and
was most anxious that you should go forward. If you feel
any interest in public life — *do go in.* You would be a tower
of strength and a powerful asset. Things are hard for poor
Patrick Hogan.

Don't let my opinion influence you but if you feel any urge
— get in. Kevin loved you and expected big things of his
faithful friend. Arthur, let me thank you for all you did for
him and for all of us.

He'll not forget you.

Your sincere friend,
Bridie O'Higgins.[90]

Arthur remained unwilling to enter public life. Instead, he
continued to be of service to those who had taken that
daunting step. His advice was at all times readily available,
both formally and informally, to those who continued the
business of State-building after Kevin O'Higgins's death.

5

Changing Times

B Y the end of the 1920s the firm of Arthur Cox & Co. was well established in Dublin business circles. The practice had expanded considerably and was very profitable. The fee income from State work alone in 1929 was in excess of £10,000.

The premises at 5 St Stephen's Green were no longer adequate for the firm's needs. In 1926 Arthur and McAreavey acquired two of the most elegant buildings on the Green, nos 42 and 43. No. 42 in particular had an intriguing history. It was once the much loved town house of Lady Ardilaun. In her time, it played host to actors, poets and playwrights who frequented her celebrated musical afternoons. Among these was W.B. Yeats whose eccentric performance on one such occasion led a fellow guest to opine that he was 'quite batty'.[91]

While the twenties were good to Arthur Cox & Co. and to Arthur himself — his appointment as Honorary Consul for Austria in 1929 further proof of his ever-increasing stature — the following decade did not start so well. For a number of years there had been signs of growing tension between Arthur and his partner. In 1930 it was decided that the partnership should be dissolved. Arthur bought out McAreavey's half share in the practice and in the premises. McAreavey took a number of files with him — mainly Probate files — thus underscoring Arthur as essentially a commercial lawyer.

Political developments were likewise not encouraging. In February 1932 the reins of power passed, more easily than had been feared, to Fianna Fáil. Arthur could no longer rely on friends in Government as a source of work. The new Government wasted little time in developing its own distinctive industrial policy. The year 1933 witnessed the birth of the Industrial Credit Corporation, the Irish Sugar Company and the Hospitals Commission. Arthur, who had been at the epicentre of the previous Government's year of initiatives in 1927, did not find his services called upon this time, the main beneficiary of the new government's legal work being the firm of John S. O'Connor & Co. This is not to suggest that there was any antipathy towards Arthur displayed by the new Government. His obvious talents were recognised as evidenced by his appointment as Law Agent to Bord na Mona, the genesis of which company can also be traced back to 1933.

Arthur, for his part, remained studiously non-party-political throughout his life. If asked his politics he would invariably reply, even much later in his days, that he was a supporter of 'the Old Irish Party'. His clients came from every political persuasion. He could count among his friends not only Patrick McGilligan, John A. Costello and later James Dillon but also Todd Andrews and Dan Breen. When John A. Costello appointed Arthur to the Senate, he sat as an Independent.

As it transpired, the new Fianna Fáil administration proved to be a far greater benefactor of Arthur's practice than the previous Government, albeit unintentionally! If continuity with the past and a consequent dislike of State intervention had been the political emblems of Cumann na nGaedheal, Fianna Fáil's stated industrial policy was one of an independent self-sufficient Irish business sector owned and controlled by Irish nationals. Foreign ownership of Irish companies was to be formally discouraged, although the necessity for foreign investment and foreign expertise was tacitly acknowledged.

The Control of Manufacturers Acts of 1932 and 1934 provided that no more than 50 per cent of the issued share capital of an Irish manufacturing company should be held by non-nationals, that two-thirds of the voting shares should be beneficially owned by Irish nationals and that a majority of directors other than the Managing Director should be Irish. A company not complying with these criteria was obliged to apply to the Minister for Industry and Commerce for a licence to conduct business. Thus, all manufacturing business was to be either Irish-owned or Irish-regulated.

The legislation proved a rather crude instrument with which to seek to regulate the ownership of Irish industry. The restrictions placed on companies operating under licence, whether in relation to the use of Irish raw materials or the employment of Irish nationals or otherwise, made the licensing procedure cumbersome and extremely unattractive. It was a much more attractive option, in many cases, to seek to avoid the need for a licence by structuring a company in such a way as to fall outside the definition of a foreign controlled business. The enactment of the Control of Manufacturers Acts provided fertile ground for lawyers and accountants retained to find loopholes in their provisions. Arthur became the architect of most of the schemes to circumscribe the legislation.

He was asked to advise a large number of foreign interests anxious to evade the attempted restriction on their ability to own and control businesses in Ireland. By a series of stratagems, over the next number of years, he drove a coach and four through the legislation. His knowledge of the provisions of the Acts and, more importantly, of the minutiae involved in circumventing their purpose, caused one commentator to say of him that he could 'put ... the Acts to music if he was inclined to.'[92] The files of the Department of Industry and Commerce bear witness to how dominant Arthur was in this area. So too do the records of the State-owned financial institution, the Industrial Credit Corporation, which invariably found Arthur's name appended to applications for funds in its early years.

Arthur's schemes relied on the creation of artificial share structures for companies. Thus, in the case of a subsidiary of a major British food processing company, the company's shares were divided into preference shares and A and B Ordinary Shares in a manner which complied with the Acts and yet left 93 per cent of the ownership and profits of the enterprise in the hands of its British parent. When the Department of Industry and Commerce challenged the arrangement, Arthur bluntly replied that his scheme was 'perfectly legal'.[93] In the case of other companies, foreign control was maintained through investment by way of loan rather than equity, while in others Irish nationals acted as trustees of shares for foreign beneficiaries.

Conscious of how much his clients depended upon the goodwill of staff in the Department, Arthur's letters were invariably polite and often laced with humour. 'Forty million Frenchmen cannot be wrong but they can be very pressing on an Irish solicitor,' he wrote in 1943 to justify his having pestered the Department for a licence for a French client.[94] As with the case of the food manufacturer, he could also be extremely curt if he felt the circumstances required it. He was intolerant of what he perceived as undue pedantry on the part of officials in interpreting the legislation and could become, on occasions, self-righteous in defending his advice against any criticism, no matter how mild.

One client for whom Arthur fought very tenaciously was Clarks, the English shoe manufacturer. During the 1930s Clarks had witnessed a serious erosion of their sales in the Irish Free State, caused mainly by the quotas introduced by the Fianna Fáil Government to protect the indigenous footwear industry. In 1937 Clarks received an approach from John Halliday & Son, an English company which had established a shoe manufacturing business in Dundalk before the advent of the legislation and which, therefore, did not require a licence. Hallidays lacked working capital and technical expertise, both of which Clarks could provide. Clarks, for its part, saw an opportunity to re-establish itself in the Irish market. Arthur was retained to advise Clarks and in February 1938 an agreement was signed whereby Clarks would provide lasts, patterns and technical expertise to Hallidays who would manufacture shoes under the Clarks brand name.

While in theory there were two separate companies, one manufacturing and the other selling, the reality was that both companies had identical boards of directors and were effectively merged. The Department sought to upset the scheme by claiming that it was merely a device to give Clarks control in a protected industry without having a licence, but Arthur's draftsmanship was such that the scheme could not be successfully attacked.[95]

The other name which monopolised the new business scene in the 1930s was Arthur's 'partner in crime', accountant

Vincent Crowley. Crowley's rise in the accountancy profession ran parallel to Arthur's progress in the legal world. He was born in 1890 a year before Arthur, and died in 1965 two months after Arthur. Shortly before Arthur Cox and John McAreavey established Arthur Cox & Co., Vincent Crowley and an equal partner, Peter Kennedy, formed Kennedy Crowley & Co. in Westmoreland Street. As with John McAreavey and Arthur, relations deteriorated between Kennedy and Crowley with Vincent Crowley buying out his partner's share in the practice.

Kennedy Crowley & Co. represented a new generation of accountants, an innovative Catholic firm perfectly positioned to take advantage of the changes wrought by independence. Like Arthur, Vincent Crowley was friendly with Patrick McGilligan, Kennedy Crowley & Co. being appointed as Auditors to the ESB. The transfer of power to Fianna Fáil did not adversely affect Vincent Crowley who, in time, became very close to Sean Lemass. While Arthur had a good working relationship with all of the accountancy firms, being particularly friendly with John Donnelly of Gardiner Donnelly, Eustace Shott of Craig Gardner, and in later years with Russell Murphy, Vincent Crowley was probably the one to whom he was closest. The firms had many clients in common and referred considerable business to each other.

Arthur and Vincent Crowley became firm friends. Crowley, like so many others, tried in vain to interest Arthur in normal social activities. When Crowley and his wife invited Arthur to dinner in the Russell Hotel, Arthur ordered, and received, a boiled egg. When they sought to encourage him to join them on a regular trip to the cinema Arthur declined, citing the dangers of forming habits! On one occasion Crowley did inveigle Arthur to join him and a friend, Ado Carton, on a trip to the cinema. Seeing the large queue outside, Crowley used his influence as Secretary of the Cinema Association to get them ahead of the line and into good seats. The film was uninspiring, causing Arthur to whisper to Carton: 'Vincent used a lot of influence to get us in. Has he enough influence to get us out again?'

Arthur Cox and Vincent Crowley were a formidable team whose contribution to the development of industrial policy in

Ireland was immeasurable. Just as the new State needed to establish its own political and economic infrastructures, so too did it need the professions to adapt to the requirements of a new age. The standards of professionalism set by Arthur Cox, Vincent Crowley and others who provided the essential back-up services without which industry could not function, played an integral part in the growth to maturity of the new Irish industrial sector. Arthur and Vincent Crowley were deeply conscious of, and took pride in, the fact that much of their work not merely enhanced their own reputations and practices but also put them in the vanguard of those dedicated to practical nationalism.

Given that the Control of Manufacturers Acts were ostensibly designed as a fundamental tenet of Fianna Fáil's industrial policy, it may seem surprising that the Government did not act swiftly to close the loopholes so adroitly exploited by Arthur and his fellow professionals. Certainly it should not have overtaxed the minds of parliamentary draughtsmen to have fashioned amendments which would have negated Arthur's efforts. There was significant pressure from native Irish businesses to have the legislation changed. The 1934 Act had sought to close off one of the more obvious loopholes in the 1932 Act, but Arthur had little difficulty in devising a new strategy to circumvent these changes.

The truth is that, far from taking umbrage at the sometimes audacious attempts to circumscribe the legislation, the Government, and certainly the Minister with responsibility for monitoring its effectiveness — Sean Lemass, then Minister for Industry and Commerce — privately welcomed the efforts of those who found ways of encouraging foreign investment in Ireland while honouring the terms of the legislation. A different Minister might have felt obliged to legislate against Arthur's schemes notwithstanding the effect which this would have had on industrial development. The pragmatic Lemass felt under no such obligation. A situation where Fianna Fáil could be seen to remain unswervingly loyal to the ideology of a self-sufficient Ireland independent of foreign influences, while at the same time Irish business could reap the obvious benefits of foreign capital and expertise, was for Lemass the best of both worlds. Publicly, he attacked the attempts to frustrate the legislation. In a Dáil debate on 28 June 1934 he stated: 'There have come during the past twelve or eighteen months certain external firms by the device of issuing preference shares which secures them their 51% of Saorstát capital, so as to avoid the necessity for the licence while, at the same time, they maintain their control in full over the factories established here. These firms are not wanted.'[96] Privately at dinner parties in Vincent Crowley's house he frequently expressed his gratitude towards, and his huge esteem for, Arthur and the work he and Crowley were doing for their country.

Official ambivalence towards the stated aim of self-sufficiency was further underlined by the involvement of ICC in many of the ventures which flew in the face of the achievement of this goal. Encouraged by Arthur who introduced many of his clients to Jim Beddy, the Chief Executive, ICC became involved either as lender or underwriter to some of the most prestigious foreign businesses in Ireland, thereby incurring the wrath of the Federation of Irish Industry which had sought even wider restrictions on foreign involvement in Irish business than those contained in the legislation.

A good example of official ambivalence to foreign investment in Ireland can be found in the case of Cement Ltd on whose Board Arthur served. The company was given the sole licence to manufacture cement in Ireland. When the Department later complained that it had been unaware that the company was substantially owned and controlled by the British company, Tunnel Cement, that company was able to point to the prospectus prepared by ICC as evidence of the fact that the Government through its agency ICC had at all times been aware of Tunnel's involvement.

It would be wrong to overstate Arthur's influence on industrial policy, to cast him as some sort of shadowy unelected figure who wielded power without responsibility. His role was always clearly defined as representing, to the best of his considerable ability, the interests of his clients. His influence was unusually great, partly because it suited Lemass that outsiders should practice that which Fianna Fáil could never preach. In analysing the key components in the maturing of industrial policy, Dr Mary Daly observed:

> Ultimately the power of government was mediated not by formal institutions, but by informal links between government and key individuals — a process made easier by Ireland's small size. Business figures such as Arthur Cox or Vincent Crowley retained close contact with the Industrial Credit Company's J.J. Beddy — a transitional figure between the state and private sectors — and Sean Lemass.[97]

To the names of Beddy and Lemass must be added that of John Leydon who was appointed as secretary of the Department of Industry and Commerce by Lemass in 1932. Leydon, born on a small farm in Co. Roscommon, first came to the attention of Lemass four years earlier when as secretary to the all-party Economics Committee he eloquently and forcefully argued the then Government's case for free trade against Lemass's protectionist creed. To Lemass's credit he chose Leydon as secretary of the Department for the stated reason that the last thing he wanted was a 'yes-man'.[98] A man of great integrity, a consummate negotiator, the inspiration behind the growth of Aer Lingus, the architect of the Anglo-Irish Trade Agreement which ended the economic war, John Leydon was in great measure responsible for the success of Lemass as Minister for Industry and Commerce. With Joseph Brennan and later J.J. McElligott in Finance, Leydon was the epitome of the new Civil Service elite. A quiet ascetic man of great authority, it was not surprising that John Leydon developed a fruitful working relationship with Arthur Cox. Arthur was in frequent direct contact with Leydon not only on behalf of clients but also as adviser and confidant to Leydon himself.

In addition to companies which sought his advice on the Control of Manufacturers legislation, Arthur was also appointed to the Boards of a number of significant domestic concerns. The two companies with which he was most closely associated were Irish Ropes and P.J. Carroll & Co. Irish Ropes was a new private company founded in 1933. It became a public company in 1946. It operated from Newbridge, Co.

Kildare as the only spinner of sisal yarns in the Free State. Arthur was Chairman of the company for nearly thirty years, guiding and counselling Michael Rigby-Jones as its managing director. On hearing of Arthur's death, Michael Rigby-Jones described him as 'truly a father to Irish Ropes'.[99]

By contrast, P.J. Carroll & Co. was an old established firm by the time Arthur joined the Board in the early 1930s. Founded in 1824, the tobacco company remained very much in the control of the Carroll family. Its ineffective marketing strategy had caused it to lose out heavily to its more aggressive rivals. The Chairman of the company, James Carroll, was an extremely autocratic man who did not encourage suggestions for change from his Board, no matter how constructive those suggestions may have been.

The only non-Carroll family directors for quite some time were Arthur and Henry Guinness of Guinness & Mahon, bankers. Over time, Arthur gained the respect of James Carroll and slowly began to orchestrate the changes which the company so badly needed. Younger faces, with new ideas, were recruited. Arthur approached Kevin McCourt who had recently been appointed as one of the four original members of the Industrial Development Authority and he became Executive Director of the company. Shortly afterwards, Arthur, Kevin McCourt and Henry Guinness persuaded a reluctant James Carroll to recruit his nephew, Don Carroll, then recently qualified as an accountant. Kevin McCourt and Don Carroll in different ways introduced considerable change to P.J. Carroll & Co. Each of them found in Arthur a wise counsel and an invaluable ally. Issues raised privately with Arthur which either of them felt were unlikely to gain the Board's approval would frequently be adopted at the next meeting, Arthur having recommended the idea to James Carroll beforehand.

Arthur was always anxious to encourage younger people and was very open to new business ideas. On one occasion, Kevin McCourt organised a market survey to assess public reaction to Carroll brands as against those of its competitors. The result of the survey was not favourable and was greeted with much scepticism by the Board. At the next meeting Arthur announced that he had been conducting his own survey. On his daily walks from his office to the Stephen's Green Club and back he had counted the discarded cigarette packets on the street and had calculated the percentage of these which represented brands owned by Carrolls. With great solemnity he revealed the precise results of his survey and declared that he would have a further bulletin for the next meeting. From that moment on, market surveys were treated with much greater reverence by the Board of P.J. Carroll & Co!

Arthur remained on the Board of Carrolls until he retired from practice in 1961. Three years later, as Fr Arthur Cox, he had the pleasant task of blessing the new premises at Grand Parade. A year before he left, he and Don Carroll negotiated a crucial deal with Rothmans which gave 40 per cent of the company to Rothmans while ensuring the future prosperity of P.J. Carroll & Co.

It is impossible to measure the extent to which Arthur's successful career was the direct result of the happy coincidence which saw him commence in practice just as some of his closest friends took over the levers of power in the new State. Certainly he benefitted not inconsiderably from State and semi-State work. The perception that he had personal access to the new State's key decision-makers clearly encouraged a number of companies to avail of his services. Yet to attribute much of his professional achievement to the good fortune of this early advantage would be to do him a great disservice. Few others, even if given a similar start, would have had the determination, the single-mindedness and the intellectual ability to exploit that advantage as Arthur did.

His success far outlasted the political careers of his contemporaries. For three decades, through changes in Government, in economic thinking, in society in general and in his own profession, he remained firmly at the top of that profession. In the three decades since he departed the Irish legal scene, no individual has come close to acquiring an equivalent status. It seems not unfair to conclude that, notwithstanding that he was in the right place at the right time, Arthur Cox would have enjoyed enormous success no matter when or where he had practised. As it was, he was always more than a mere practitioner of the law. He was a businessman, a broker, an innovator and, above all else, a problem solver.

He became also, in time, something of a national institution. Profiles of him appeared in the newspapers, which, while not always entirely flattering, invariably paid homage to his pre-eminence. The most unconventional profile appeared in the September 1955 edition of *Labour,* a newspaper published by the Dublin Regional Council of the Labour Party. It was the only profile which Arthur bothered to keep. It read:

Meet Mr Arthur Cox

No publicity seeker is Senator Arthur Cox. Yet he wields power to an extent that few others do. Not as the principal spokesman of the employers on the Law Clerks' Joint Labour Committee. Nor as senior partner of the largest law firm in Ireland. Nor as a member of the Senate to which he was nominated by the Taoiseach, Mr Costello. But as chairman or director of at least fifteen important companies employing thousands of workers and with a combined capital of several million pounds. To his offices in St Stephen's Green come regular reports on the progress of scores of companies for which his firm acts as law agents or advisers. But legal work is a part only of Mr Cox's activities. For this retiring, reticent gentleman is one of the big names in Irish industry. The quiet-spoken Senator is a lord of the boardroom.

Advice

'Clear it with Cox,' is advice that might well be given to visiting industrialists anxious to set up associate companies here. Industrial finance is his meat and Stock Exchange quotations his wine. Adaptable might be Arthur's second name. He need must be (sic). Not everyone is capable of being versed in the production and financial problems of nearly a score of companies. The products of these companies range from nylons to disinfectants, from cigarettes to cement, from ropes to transformers and from wallboard to watches. His versatility amazes his associates and confounds his rivals.

Today he may be discussing the production of three-phase transformers with George Cauchie of Ateliers des Construcions Electriques de Charleroi for both are directors of A.C.E.C. (Ireland) Ltd. Tomorrow, maybe, he must talk over the marketing of wallboard with Eric Vansittart Bowater, chairman of the giant Bowater Paper Corporation and a fellow-director of Irish Wallboard. Later he may attend a board meeting of Cement Ltd with Mr N.M. Jenson of Tunnel Portland Cement, London, or join his fellow-senator, Howard Eustace Guinness in the boardroom of Irish Ropes.

Yes, Mr Cox's industrial interests are many and varied. Here are just a few of the other firms with which he is associated — P.J. Carroll (Sweet Afton), Browne and Nolan (publishers), Rolex Watch Co. of Éire, Jeyes Sanitary Compounds, Bradmola Mills (hosiery), Gestetner Ltd, Montagu Burton Tailoring Co.

Workers

From Roscrea to Ballaghaderreen, Dundalk to Waterford, Newbridge to Drogheda and, of course, in Dublin, thousands of Irish workers who have never heard of Mr Cox are helping to swell his bank account.

A busy man is Mr Cox. Wealthy, too, for his companies thrive, their balance sheets healthy, their profits booming.[100]

Apart from corporate work, Arthur's practice developed in other directions during the 1930s. In 1933 the firm was asked to defend a doctor sued by the parents of a young boy who claimed she had been negligent in operating on the boy's arm. Although the doctor was uninsured, the Medical Defence Union, which insured a large number of doctors, took a keen interest in the case and was so impressed by the manner in which the firm handled it that Arthur Cox & Co. became solicitors to the MDU in Ireland.

6

An Eccentric Genius

ON 5 August 1940, Arthur married Brigid O'Higgins; the ceremony took place in the Church of the Sacred Heart, Donnybrook. That they married caused considerable surprise, though Arthur's friends were more fascinated by how he ever plucked up sufficient courage to propose (if, in fact, he did!).

In the thirteen years since Kevin O'Higgins's death Arthur had kept in regular touch with his widow and with their two daughters, Maev and Una. Maev recalls, at the age of six, accompanying her mother to 'Mr Cox's office' and being delighted to find a photograph of herself on the mantelpiece and to be invited to recite her party-piece into Arthur's dictaphone. Three years later she sat with her mother and Una on the balcony of the Cox home at Merrion Square watching the Papal Legate driving in state to the opening of the Eucharistic Congress.

The arrangements for the wedding were clouded in secrecy. Arthur was anxious that any fuss might be made. Close friends were not informed until shortly before the event. Typical of the form of notice was the following letter sent to one of Arthur's friends: 'I thought I should let you know that very shortly Mrs O'Higgins and I are to be married. There is to be no announcement, no one will be there, and there will I hope be neither photographs in the papers nor, on any account, presents. Mother is, I think, very pleased. We mean to make Carraig Breac and no. 26 joint bases, so that she may not be lonely. Please mention this to no one.'[101] The sense of secrecy was heightened by their decision to marry at 6.30 am on a Bank Holiday Monday, although a number of Arthur's colleagues cruelly suggested that the time was chosen so as to interfere, to the least possible extent, with Arthur's work schedule! George O'Brien was best man, Maev was bridesmaid.

After a short holiday, Arthur, his new wife and his two step-daughters settled down to life at Carraig Breac, a magnificent home on The Baily, in Howth, with a panoramic view of Dublin Bay. He had bought Carraig Breac in 1936 from Sir William Stokes. The house, which was originally built in 1853, had a very substantial garden which Brigid, with the help of a gardener who lived in a lodge beside the main house, struggled to maintain.

The house was near where the tram to and from Dublin stopped at Baily Cross. Arthur travelled to work each day by tram unless, as often was the case, he got a lift from his neighbours the Forsyths. He became Chairman of the local Fairy Hill Hospital, but apart from a considerable contribution to the hospital's development he had little involvement with local matters. While his workload caused him to spend relatively little time at Carraig Breac, Maev and Una were actively encouraged by 'Uncle Arthur', (the title which replaced 'Mr Cox'), to have lots of young friends to stay. Between friends of the two girls, various relations and even clients, Carraig Breac was rarely without a visitor.

Brigid Cox was a friendly outgoing person who had not allowed the tragedy of her first husband's death cause her to be bitter or morose. The pretty young teacher, Brigid Cole, who had captivated Kevin O'Higgins, was a strikingly elegant woman when she married his friend. In contrast to the dark gloomy atmosphere of Merrion Square, Brigid's cheerful disposition ensured that Carraig Breac was a bright and happy home. She proved a tremendous support and loyal friend to Arthur, accepting his idiosyncrasies with amused forbearance. Not least of these was his habit of continuing to refer to her in public as 'Mrs O'Higgins' throughout their married life, in terms which gave not inconsiderable amusement to onlookers such as when he would announce at a dinner party: 'It's time Mrs O'Higgins and I went to bed.'

But what of Arthur as a person? In his introduction to the subject of his M.A. thesis, Philip Massinger, Arthur observed that Carlyle, when writing his *History of the French Revolution,* kept portraits of the chief characters on his desk so that he could better understand the men and the movements for which they stood. A photograph of Arthur Cox in the 1940s or 1950s provides an interesting picture of him: the suit unkempt and ill-fitting, the waistcoat wrongly buttoned, the lapel dotted with ash, the collar turned up, the tie askew, the hair unruly, the teeth uneven, and illuminating this sartorial disaster, an impudent but kindly smile.

His dress sense — or at least the lack of it — is that which is immediately recalled by those who knew him well but not intimately. He appeared to revel in his own lack of style where clothes were concerned. It was even thought by some that the Arthur Cox 'look' was intentional, that he purposely undid his tie and ruffled his hair before appearing in public. So renowned was he for his shabby appearance that in Dublin circles an incorrectly buttoned waist coat became known as an 'Arthur Cox'.

He certainly did not live up to the high standard of dress set for himself in his diary entry for 22 November 1913: 'Ordered two suits from Walkey. Expensive: but I mean to be dapper, like Samuel Pepys.' James Meenan relates that when, at the beginning of the Second World War, George O'Brien felt it necessary to buy two new suits, Arthur self-mockingly remarked: 'George must expect a Thirty Years War',[102] although others recall the story as George telling a rare joke at Arthur's expense.

The parts not caught by the photographs were no better. On his feet he wore shoes with the laces — often pieces of string — invariably open, until later in his life when his wife discovered the joys of slip-on footwear. He was known to wear carpet slippers to important meetings. On his head he wore a hat which, almost from the first day he wore it, looked as if it had seen better days. On one visit to London to meet important contacts in the British electricity industry his two travelling companions, horrified by the condition of Arthur's hat, decided it was imperative that he be persuaded to acquire a new one before the meeting. One of them announced that he wished to buy a new hat for himself and so all three headed to a nearby shop. The first checked out the hats, expressed himself satisfied with a particularly fine one and purchased it.

The second, in a further effort to drum up enthusiasm for the art of hat-purchasing, proceeded to acquire an impressive piece of headgear. The two, having purchased hats, (neither of which was needed) turned to Arthur and said 'Would you not consider buying one, Arthur?' Arthur removed his own battered specimen, studied it closely, caressed it fondly, dusted it gently and replied: 'It will last me a few more years.' Thus ended the shopping!

Arthur's unusual appearance was dismissed by many as just another eccentricity. The label 'eccentric' is one which is almost synonymous with Arthur Cox. His style of dress contributed in no small measure to this, but so too did his general approach to life. He never drank alcohol and would not even sample sherry trifle. He ate very little. Breakfast usually consisted of a cup of coffee and a bun. Lunch was typically the same, food not being allowed to interfere with his lunch-time passion for completing *The Times* crossword with extraordinary speed and for indulging his insatiable appetite for detective stories. For one accomplished in French, Italian, Spanish and German, with a First Class Honours M.A. in English Literature, who owned a library which boasted first editions of Joyce, Yeats and O'Casey, and who read Goethe and Schiller in their original texts, it was another extraordinary facet of his being — invariably attributed to that overused description of eccentric — that he adored popular detective novels. He devoured Raymond Chandler and Agatha Christie, sometimes interrupting a consultation to pick up an overturned piece of fiction and read a page, explaining to a startled client that he had just reached a good part! His favourite was Erle Stanley Gardner. Perhaps he imagined himself in his fantasies as an Irish Perry Mason!

Dinner, to the regular exasperation of his wife, was treated with no greater respect or enthusiasm than the earlier meals of the day. In an effort to encourage him to eat, Brigid arranged with Mills on Merrion Row to bring afternoon tea each day to his office. After a number of days they telephoned her and asked politely if it would be possible to recover some of their trays which Arthur had stacked, untouched, on top of a mound of files. In later years he did venture out to Mills, the Swiss Chalet or Jurys for a cup of tea in the evening.

His lack of interest in food and drink, while inevitably resulting in his frame being decidedly scrawny, did not give rise to any deficiency in his energy for work. It may be that he secretly indulged his liking for chocolate — particularly Fry's chocolate cream bars — more frequently than he admitted! His teeth certainly bore witness to and were victims of his unhealthy diet.

He was socially very shy. He was uneasy in large crowds and uncomfortable at small talk in a social setting. His shyness was sometimes mistaken for aloofness or rudeness but neither of these descriptions was fair. At worst he was difficult and uncommunicative, although on one occasion in the Stephen's Green Club he refused an invitation to dinner from someone of whom he did not approve by curtly replying: 'I will be dining with my dog.'

His reluctance to engage in small talk was derived partly from his abhorrence of snobbery. It was also influenced by his innate caution. The topics and scandals which amused and fascinated his neighbours and friends were frequently those which had passed across his desk that day. A less discreet person might have been tempted to enthral a dinner party or two by adding a few further intimate details to their knowledge of the most recent public drama. For Arthur, his office was his confessional and anyone who sought his advice — whether formally or informally, on a legal matter or otherwise — could be assured of total confidentiality. His silence at dinners or parties (which he attended infrequently) was often imposed by this duty of confidentiality which he owed to those who entrusted him with their concerns.

While Arthur's reluctance to involve himself in the normal social graces may well have been caused by a mixture of shyness and caution, it was also assisted by the indulgence of those who knew him. Others might have been cajoled or forced to take a more active part in social matters or might have been ignored and removed from future invitation lists. Arthur was always given the benefit of the doubt. He could turn up late to dinner because his host recognised that, for Arthur, work always took precedence. He could sit or stand apart from the general gathering because he was assumed to be musing on some complicated legal conundrum. He could say nothing, eat little and leave early because 'That's Arthur!' (or 'Sir Arthur' as he was irreverently known to some of his friends). Everyone else was obliged to adapt their habits to suit him. There was no compromise, no gesture to normal social etiquette, on Arthur's part. His reputation as the antithesis of a social animal earned him the dubious distinction of being the only member of the Stephen's Green Club profiled in its recent 150 years celebration history to be described as not really 'clubbable'.[103]

His refusal to contribute to chit-chat or gossip should not be taken as inferring that he had no interest in what was going on in Dublin or further afield. Just as he would not betray his secrets, he delighted in knowing them. His practice as a lawyer made him a supreme listener. He could persuade the most reticent person to disclose his life story without having to utter more than a few words himself. He revelled in the notion that his contempories knew he was in the know but would not share that knowledge. When he did choose to confide in somebody, he liked to create an atmosphere of high drama before doing so. During the time Terence de Vere White was researching his biography of Kevin O'Higgins, Arthur asked him to come to Carraig Breac. No explanation was given. As soon as they sat down in the drawing room, Arthur said: 'I hear you've been asking whether Michael Collins knew who shot Sir Henry Wilson?' 'I have', replied an intrigued de Vere White. A lengthy silence ensued. Then Arthur got up, closed one window, then the next, drew each set of drapes in turn, closed the door, circled the large room a few times and with the aura of conspiracy finely tuned, sat down again and whispered 'Collins knew, but you must never tell anybody!'[104]

Many years later, when he had decided to become a priest, de Vere White and others were treated to similar performances as one by one each of Arthur's friends was told the news and then sworn to secrecy — this when the solicitors' offices of Fitzwilliam Square and St Stephen's Green were already buzzing with reports of Arthur's imminent departure from their midst.

Like many shy people, Arthur felt most at ease with people who simply did not understand or recognise shyness in others. The chattier the person was, the more Arthur liked to be in his or her company. Two silent people together can be a recipe for social disaster and Arthur, although he did absolutely nothing to change it, did at least recognise his own shortcoming. It is understandable, therefore, that Arthur felt most relaxed in the company of children and young people. He was surprisingly good with children and loved to show off his collection of tricks at any available opportunity. With children Arthur was free to be himself, released from the constraints which adult social etiquette imposed on people in his position.

There is a sense in which Arthur's love of children in his later life served to fill some of the voids in his own childhood. As a young child he was very much a loner, remaining silent until he was four, preferring to stay indoors drawing pictures and reading books while Aedan enjoyed outdoor pursuits. Life at Merrion Square was lonely at times, with plenty of opportunities for Arthur to invent his own games but with no audience on which to try them out. Children who are especially gifted and academically competitive frequently long for the freedom which simple childish games and puzzles can bring. Arthur had a strong desire to be adventurous, to be 'captain of the school team', but his innate caution prevented him. As one friend remarked, it is most unlikely that Arthur ever jumped over a five-bar gate. Throughout his life there survived in him an endearing childlike quality, a youthful anarchic streak, which frequently showed its face and which, in light of the seriousness expected of a person in his position with the enormous responsibilities he was obliged to bear, served to allow him a release he so clearly needed while adding to the eccentricity by which he was superficially and almost universally recognised.

He spent many happy hours as an adult teaching his cousin Aileen's children card tricks or worse how to cheat at cards, slipping in unannounced through the back door of their home at Wilton Place to share with them his latest piece of mischief before slipping out again. His favourite party piece was mirror-writing. When Una was in boarding-school, he

wrote letters to her in this way so that they were only readable
when held up to a mirror. To show how he had mastered the
technique (and, it must be admitted, to show off) Arthur once
entertained a colleague by completing *The Times* crossword in
this fashion. On another occasion he proved to Vincent
Crowley that a cheque can be written on any form of paper
by writing the details on the back of a postage stamp and
promptly getting it cashed in a nearby bank!

Arthur's passion for dogs was also childlike in its intensity.
Each one was treated as a full member of the family. Even
family wedding photographs invariably included a dog. Each
was buried with great solemnity in the garden, with Arthur
composing a suitable poem for the occasion. As he
dismounted the Howth tram each evening, he would be met
by his latest dog friend. He liked to imagine them telling him
their life stories and would invent appropriate dialogues. One
dog called 'Val' became 'Sir Valentine' and wrote to Una in
boarding-school of his latest doings, causing much
consternation among the nuns who intercepted her mail.

Arthur didn't drive a car. At one stage he owned a Dodge
but, co-ordination not being a strong suit, he travelled most
of his life by tram or taxi. Curiously, he had a pilot's licence,
the fruit of lessons taken at a young age. He had a half-share
in a boat but pressures of work rarely allowed him to sail or
to avail of his membership of the Royal Irish Yacht Club. He
even had a racehorse named after him by a grateful client,
but asked that the name be changed when he became
annoyed at colleagues telephoning after races in which the
horse competed to enquire if he was feeling tired!

He loved to walk and was a familiar sight strolling around
St Stephen's Green. The Green was a much more sociable
place than it is today. Nowadays it serves, to a great extent, as
a pleasant place to pass through for people still employed in
Georgian Dublin who wish to eat or shop in the plastic desert
that it is now Grafton Street, a short cut for those whose lives
are ruled by fixed lunch times and busy deadlines which do
not permit of idle chat or amiable loitering.

In Arthur's time the Green was an oasis where time stood
still and the next appointment would simply have to wait if

one chanced upon a friend, a colleague, or a 'character' — as Arthur was known in the Green to casual acquaintances. The tall angular figure in shabby attire, his beloved hat on his head, his nose stuck inside a Gardner or Christie, was a regular sight for Green habitués. Colleagues would approach him for free advice, friends to enquire after the health of his aged mother, his own health or the state of the nation. Arthur would nod, smile, doff his hat if the enquirer was a lady, and say little if anything, always listening intently to the latest news. When his companion would have exhausted his or her entire vocabulary on the chosen subject Arthur would utter, or more accurately, mutter a sentence or two of pertinent if whimsical comment and then, his companion happy, he would return to his book, his chocolate or his office.

On other occasions, to people he knew well, Arthur would make the first approach, gesturing them to stop with a silent twitch of his hand, before delivering some off-beat comment on an unexpected topic, a writer, art, religion; the gem of wisdom delivered, he would be on his way before any response could be given. He once stopped a colleague in the Green and asked: 'Do you know how the great portrait painters study their subjects?' 'No', came the bemused reply. 'Like this', announced Arthur, bending over and looking back through his outstretched legs before continuing on his journey.

If Arthur Cox, at social gatherings or wandering through St Stephen's Green, provided good entertainment value to those he met along the way, it was nothing compared to the performance which sometimes greeted a client who came to his office seeking advice. A consultation with Arthur at 42–43 St Stephen's Green was not merely a legal ritual — it could often be a piece of theatre.

The persons in charge of the door at this particular theatre — the keepers of the gate — were for a long time two formidable sisters, the Miss Geoghegans. Ushered by Miss Agnes Geoghegan into a small room near Arthur's own office, an unsuspecting client might find himself waiting for a very long time before seeing Arthur. Modern concepts of time management would not have suited him. His office was a timeless zone where stories unfolded and problems were solved at a speed entirely dictated by himself.

When he was ready to perform, the principal actor would guide his audience to his office. Arthur's melodramas did not follow any set pattern. Act I might well see Arthur on his knees digging for a file with his back turned to his audience. It might consist of Arthur introducing a quite irrelevant topic which his gallery was expected to address. It might witness him searching his person for a lit cigarette which he had dropped. It might simply comprise a few minutes of silence punctuated by occasional incomprehensible murmurs. The scene set, Arthur would, almost unnoticed, move the drama to Act II, the business of the day.

One visit by a set of wealthy foreign businessmen who had been advised by their own lawyers to go to Arthur Cox for assistance is illustrative of how the plot in an Arthur play would frequently develop. Having survived the apparent irrelevance of Act I, the visitors enthusiastically outlined, in extraordinary detail, the difficulties they were encountering in Ireland. Without warning, Arthur rose from his chair and as if in a trance began to walk around the table. The visitors continued as if nothing had happened. Then the quiet mumbling began, the hands started to shake, the eyes closed, then opened. Apparently oblivious to his audience, Arthur turned his back on them and stared out the window. One of the visitors unused to such behaviour, tried to get Arthur's attention but to no avail. Suddenly, Arthur returned to the table. The relief on the audience's faces was quickly shattered for instead of rejoining them Arthur began to circle the table, sometimes pausing behind one of them as if to speak, but then heading off again. To their horror, the show was only beginning.

On one circuit of the table he left the room altogether, departing stage right into the filing-room which connected with his own room. From the filing-room, he visited the nearby strong-room before returning to an audience of bewildered and annoyed clients who, tired of trying to grab his attention as he went on his circuits, had resolved to leave this madman whom it had been their misfortune to consult.

Just as the last of the audience packed his papers in to his briefcase, Arthur came and stood behind him. 'Gentlemen', said Arthur, 'this is your problem,' and he proceeded to summarise with amazing clarity the root of their difficulties. The audience began to relax, astounded by how the madman who had seemed to ignore everything they had said, could summarise in a few sentences the critical elements of their concerns. 'And this', continued Arthur, 'is what we shall do,' and with similar incisiveness he outlined a coherent strategy for resolving their problems. Three days later the problems were indeed solved and a firm of London lawyers was profusely thanked for having recommended such a 'genius'!

A Texan lawyer, who had a similar experience, when asked nervously by the local accountant who had recommended Arthur what he thought of Ireland's leading solicitor, replied: 'This sure is the first time I've seen a Rolls Royce engine on a Ford chassis!'

Many clients testify to similar if not identical experiences: Arthur lying on the floor, Arthur playing with his shoes, Arthur giving dictation to secretaries on a totally different case, even Arthur finding it necessary during a meeting to go outside and feed the birds! At first glance it seems extraordinary that anyone who behaved in such a bizarre manner could have managed not only to retain the loyalty of his clients but to gain a pre-eminent status in his profession. The explanation for this lies in the fact that while most clients testified to his being eccentric, all testified in much stronger terms to his genius. While 'eccentric' is the adjective which most readily comes to mind, 'brilliant' is the one which, on reflection, invariably is seen as much more appropriate. As a lawyer, as a negotiator, as a strategist, as a pillar of commercial common sense and as a weapon to have in one's armoury, Arthur Cox for over three decades had no equal. His eccentricities were never allowed to get in the way of his professional performance. Though he affected a haphazard dotty image, Arthur was at all times totally in control.

As well as being brilliant he was also very shrewd. He was quick to identify any weaknesses in his opposition and to exploit them ruthlessly. He was always anxious to force his opponent to start a negotiation, staunchly believing that this made it easier for him to gain concessions when he would eventually deign to address the meeting. At one meeting in London with equally crafty Scottish bankers who were owed substantial money by his client, Arthur spent the first ten minutes pretending to read with the aid of a magnifying glass a document he already knew by heart until, finally, the bankers blinked and began to talk. When they finished Arthur treated them to a further silence before putting them out of their misery and getting his client out of a mess.

He was addicted to his work. Before his marriage his entire life revolved around the office where he regularly worked long past midnight. His marriage and the move to Howth made some difference, though little enough. Even if he returned to Howth for dinner, he would quite frequently travel back to Stephen's Green later in the evening. Saturdays, Sundays, even Christmas Day were always spent, at least in part, in the office.

His workload, throughout his career, was enormous. He was incapable of turning away work and was always annoyed to find that an interesting assignment had gone to a competitor. His lot was not made any easier by his inability to delegate and by his disorganised style. While he had working with him people well capable of sharing part of his burden, Arthur found it difficult to hand over a case fully to anyone other than a very senior colleague. One result of this was that, although there was always a significant number of apprentices in the office at any given time, they were given very little responsibility.

Not only did Arthur have difficulty in delegating work within the office: he rarely even came in contact with most of his staff. Communication was invariably by way of polite notes. Several people who worked with the firm claim never to have set eyes on him! Empty coffee cups would be left by him outside his door, the only clear evidence that he was present. On one occasion, the apprentices, whose room was above Arthur's, decided to fill in the time by playing football. Shortly afterwards, a note arrived enquiring: 'Who let in the horses?'

His room was chaotic. It was constantly filled with smoke, due not only to his chain-smoking of cigarettes supplied by P.J. Carroll & Co., and in later life a pipe, but also to his practice of using the upturned bowls of standard lamps as ashtrays, so that at times they resembled Olympic torches. Every available square inch of furniture and floor was littered with files and papers. His filing system consisted of throwing correspondence into already heaving bundles on the floor. Miraculously, he could always extract from the rubble the papers he needed. The trick was to persuade Arthur to dictate a letter or document on the spot, lest the relevant file would return to the debris. He was so busy that, if he failed to deal with a matter immediately, it could be forgotten for some time.

He had an extraordinary ability to dictate the most complicated of documents *extempore*. His letters were short and always to the point. He liked to say that he only wrote long letters when he did not have time to compose short ones! When the mood took him, his letters were also very entertaining. To one client who enjoyed playing bridge, Arthur summarised his advice on a commercial problem in the form of a bridge game. When a client sent a gentle reminder to Arthur that he had failed to deal with a complicated Trust and cautioned that 'neither of us is getting any younger,' Arthur replied: 'You seem to have overlooked the fact that I will live to be 150 and will be killed on a flight to the moon by an interplanetary missile (a reliable fortune teller told me this).' In response to a tax query which required Arthur to state whether his mother (then approaching ninety) was younger or older than sixty-five, Arthur retorted: 'I would not like to ask mother her age. It would only worry and fluster her. However, if my brother were alive today he would be 65. This seems to me conclusive.'

His whimsical approach also frequently applied to the question of fees. He had little interest in money per se. Although disclaiming any knowledge of its value, he was keenly aware of its worth. He was also deeply conscious of his own worth. His approach to billing was haphazard and many people, particularly charities who benefitted from his advice over many years, were never charged for it. He was always willing to give his advice free of charge if a particular situation merited it. Yet he was not reluctant to seek significant fees if he felt they were warranted. The amount sought from an international airline company for advice in relation to a public enquiry into a crash was such as to encourage three executives from the company to fly to Dublin to voice their concerns to Arthur's face. Having listened politely to them, Arthur whispered: 'If you can't afford the fee, it's alright.' The psychology was superb. What the airline company could not afford was the suggestion that it might be unable to meet its obligations. The executives went straight from Arthur's office to the Bank of Ireland next door, purchased a bank draft, and presented it to him with a speech of gratitude for all his work!

Another client received a bill which he felt was modest having regard to the amount of work which Arthur had done on his behalf. He invited Arthur to increase the amount. Arthur took back the original bill, added an extra nought at the end, and returned it! One client who asked Arthur to set out in writing the likely fees he would charge got instead the following: 'It is all together too complicated to give you an estimate. The best I can do is to say that I fear and hope they will be enormous. This is a guess, not a guarantee.'

Eccentric but very brilliant. Brilliant but very eccentric. It is remarkable how these two phrases dominate the memories of those who knew Arthur Cox. No-one seems quite sure in retrospect which is the more apposite. Did Arthur seem peculiarly eccentric because of his unique talent or was he simply assumed to be brilliant because he was so extra-ordinarily eccentric? Rather than one being the progenitor of the other, the evidence would suggest that these two facets of his character led a symbiotic existence. What is certain is that Arthur made no attempt to discourage either opinion being held of him.

For all his superficial eccentricity in matters of dress and social graces, Arthur was essentially very orthodox in his attitudes and beliefs. He remained, at all times, an unswerving believer in the mores and values of the conservative Catholic professional class of the new independent State. Though innovative in his approach to solving problems he was most certainly not radical in his ideology. His interest in art and literature was similarly conventional. He had little time for

Arthur's parents, Dr Michael Cox and Mrs Lily Cox, in formal attire for Dr Cox's inauguration as a member of the Irish Privy Council, 1911.

Arthur with his elder brother Aedan.

The cluttered splendour of the drawing room at 26 Merrion Square.

Arthur and his wife Brigid shortly after their marriage in August 1940.

Arthur and canine friend.

Arthur boards the tram at The Baily in Howth.

Carraig Breac, The Baily.

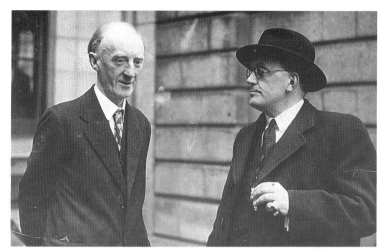

Arthur with James Dillon TD at the Four Courts.

The Board of P.J. Carroll & Company Ltd, December 1959.
Back row (*left to right*): J.G. McKinley, H.E. Guinness, W.J. Carroll, C.A. Carroll, H.W. Kennedy. Front row (*left to right*): Arthur, James Carroll, Don Carroll.

Arthur, as President of the Incorporated Law Society, and Brigid join with the President of Ireland, Sean T. O Ceallaigh and with Mrs O Ceallaigh, to greet the Taoiseach, Eamon de Valera, at a Garden Party at Aras an Uachtarain, to open the centenary celebration of the Incorporated Law Society, 1952.

Arthur and Brigid greet Arthur's college friend, Chief Justice Conor Maguire, at the Charter Centenary Dinner of the Incorporated Law Society at the Gresham Hotel, 28 May 1952.

The Shaw connection (from left): Arthur, Brother Cormac OFM, Gabriel Pascal and Dan Breen TD.

The President of Ireland, Sean T. O Ceallaigh, Professor Michael O'Malley and Arthur, at the reception following the wedding of Professor O'Malley's son Eoin to Arthur's step-daughter Una in 1952.

Fr Arthur Cox on departure from Dublin for Northern Rhodesia, with his step-daughter Una, her husband Eoin O'Malley, and their sons Kevin and Eoin, August 1964.

Fr Frank O'Neill SJ and Fr Arthur Cox in Rome, en route to Northern Rhodesia, August 1964.

'new' artists or writers and flatly refused to pander to changing trends. His orthodoxy, to a large extent, was his eccentricity — he remained not merely politically but also philosophically a member of the Old Party long after such allegiances had been rendered obsolete.

The true extent of his brilliance is more difficult to evaluate. Genius is relative not absolute and Arthur's academic record and professional achievements certainly bear favourable comparison with any other similar product of this country. But just as there remains the suspicion that a fair proportion of his eccentricity was contrived, there is also a sense in which he skilfully masked any shortcomings in his intellectual capability. He was never reluctant to show off his ability in an area in which he felt supremely confident, and he had sufficient knowledge on a wide range of subjects to be able to bluff his way through most encounters. He occasionally remarked that it mattered little whether an opinion was right or wrong provided it was asserted with manifest authority. He refused to indulge in debate on any topic on which he might not emerge winner and was openly dismissive of the merits of writers or artists whose work he had not closely studied. If these stratagems succeeded in clouding the issue as to the true breadth of his knowledge on particular subjects, there can be no gainsaying his effectiveness as a commercial lawyer or the outstanding success of his professional career.

7

Famous and Infamous Cases

W HILE advising large businesses on matters of commercial
law preoccupied Arthur throughout his career, he was
always pleased to dabble in other areas, particularly where the
case or the client had a high profile. Although the firm, in
common with the other firms specialising in commercial
matters, did not get involved in routine criminal law cases,
Arthur enthusiastically seized the opportunity to represent
the defendant in a sensational murder trial when the father
of the accused asked him to act. The firm's only other
recorded venture into criminal law was an appearance in the
District Court by Arthur in the 1920s when one of his
secretaries, with strong Republican sympathies, was charged
with having an illegal revolver in her handbag!

A Murder Trial

On the night of 23 January 1948 four young friends joined
other revellers at the Killiney Golf Club Dress Dance which
was held at the Royal Marine Hotel in Dun Laoghaire. They
were Miss Maureen Macken and her sister Imelda of Dalkey,
Mr Bobby Robinson of Glenageary (a son of the prominent
Dublin solicitor, T.P. Robinson) and Mr Ronald Ernest Brain,
a native of New Zealand. While at the dance, Maureen
Macken was approached by Lieutenant Harry Cotton, a
twenty-five-year-old officer in the Irish army. Cotton and
Maureen Macken had been keeping company for a number
of years. Their relationship ended in the Autumn of 1947 and
in December, a month before the dance, she had written to
Cotton to say that she wished the New Year to start well for
him but, though fond of him, she did not love him and could
not marry him.

After dancing with Cotton, Maureen sat on a settee with Bobby Robinson who was now her boyfriend. Cotton approached them, whereupon Robinson insisted that she choose between himself and Cotton, to which she replied that she intended to marry Bobby Robinson. Cotton tried to push Robinson who shrugged him off. Robinson, Brain, Maureen and Imelda Macken then left and went to the Macken home at Darwin House, Dalkey.

At 4.30 am they heard a loud knock on the door. All four answered it and saw Harry Cotton, still in his dress-suit, with his right hand in his pocket. He was clearly in an excited state and asked to see Maureen Macken alone. He was shown into the study where Robinson refused to leave. Words were exchanged. Imelda Macken went to call her father. Cotton produced a revolver and shot Bobby Robinson. He then turned the gun on Ronald Brain. Both men were killed. Cotton left the house and returned by tug to the yacht on which he was living at the time. He was arrested at 8.30 am and charged with the murder of Robinson and Brain.

Later that morning Harry Cotton's father, an executive in the Dublin Gas Company, contacted Arthur who immediately visited Cotton in jail. Arthur represented him in the District Court and then retained P.J. Roe SC and Desmond Bell SC for the hearing which commenced in the Central Criminal Court on 8 March 1948.[105]

At the opening of the trial the Defence made an application that Cotton was unfit to plead. Expert medical evidence was called which indicated that Cotton had no clear recollection of the shootings and had an attitude of 'strained, good-natured detachment' from the tragedy and from his circumstances in Mountjoy. The jury failed to agree on whether Cotton was fit to stand trial. A second jury was empanelled to consider the same issue. On this occasion, Mr Roe announced that he intended to take the unusual step of calling Arthur to give evidence. He said that Arthur, 'a solicitor of great experience', had met with Cotton on the day of his arrest and later at the District Court and had concluded that there was no point in seeking to take instructions from him. Arthur and Counsel then met Cotton at Mountjoy but, once more, no instructions could be taken as the entire interview consisted of a monologue by Cotton on irrelevant matters. Sir John Esmonde, for the Prosecution, objected to Arthur seeking to give an opinion on Cotton's mental state and it was therefore decided not to call him.

The second jury decided that Cotton was fit to plead and a third jury was chosen to consider the charges of murder brought against him. There was clearly no doubt that Cotton had killed the two men, so the Defence had no option but to direct all its efforts towards obtaining a verdict of guilty but insane. Witnesses described in harrowing detail the effect on Cotton of an explosion at the Glen of Imaal in 1941. A mine exploded killing fourteen men and injuring many others including Cotton who lost an eye and had serious internal injuries caused partly by the bone of another man being blown into his stomach. He spent a year in hospital and evidence was given that his sanity was clearly affected by the horrific accident. Further evidence was given of how he had become irritable in the months before the killings, how he cried at the dance and how he showed no remorse or even understanding after he shot Robinson and Brain.

Cotton, for his part, cut an odd figure in Court, appearing uninterested and vague, displaying to his lawyers less concern about the outcome of his case than about the result of the Rugby International between Ireland and Wales which gained Ireland its first Triple Crown in fifty years and which was played on the day his Counsel opened his defence. The jury took less than an hour to return the verdict for which the Defence had pleaded. It was a successful conclusion to the criminal law practice of Arthur Cox & Co.

Years later Arthur was nearly retained to act in one of the longest running criminal law sagas in Irish legal history when Dr Paul Singer was charged with fraud arising out of the collapse of Shanahan Stamp Auctions. The mercurial Singer retained Arthur on behalf of the company to petition the High Court for its winding up, Arthur making the somewhat disingenuous public statement that the application to wind up the company did not 'necessarily mean that it was bankrupt'! When criminal charges were commenced against Singer he retained a different firm of solicitors. Arthur, none

the less, amused himself by telling friends and colleagues that
he had once acted for 'Singer's Owing Machine'.

The KLM Public Inquiry

On 5 September 1954 at 2.30 am a Lockheed Super
Constellation owned by KLM Royal Dutch Airlines took off
from Shannon Airport for Gander Airport in Canada with a
crew of ten, forty-eight passengers and cargo aboard. Take-off
appeared normal but forty seconds later the plane had
ditched into the River Shannon. Three crew members and
twenty-five passengers lost their lives and the aircraft was
totally written off. The deaths were caused by asphyxiation
from petrol fumes in the cabin. The tragedy provoked an
enormous public reaction, particularly when it became
known that there had been an inordinate delay in
commencing the rescue operation. Indeed, it was not until
5.12 am, nearly three hours after the crash, when a survivor
in great distress alerted a fire station, that formal rescue
procedures were put in place.

The Minister for Industry and Commerce ordered a public
inquiry under the Chairmanship of Mr Justice Teevan. It
began on 29 November 1954 at the King's Inns at Henrietta
Street and sat for twenty-eight days. The Minister, the
Attorney General, Shannon Airport, Aer Lingus, Sabena
Airlines, Irish Shell Limited and the Dutch Government were
each represented at the hearings. So too, of course, was KLM
which inevitably was very much in the spotlight in relation to
the safety of its aircraft and the competence of its crew. KLM
engaged Arthur to advise them and he, in turn, retained the
services of Dick McGonigal SC, William O'Brien FitzGerald
SC and Tommy McLaughlin.

The Inquiry considered, in minute detail, the events
surrounding the tragedy of Flight 633X. It was essential, from
KLM's viewpoint, that as much blame as possible be placed
on the delayed rescue. Counsel representing the airport
authorities sought to call into question the safety procedures
on the aircraft and the reactions of the Captain when he
became aware of the difficulties. This lead to very robust
cross-examination on each side and a host of expert witnesses

on weather patterns, rescue procedures and staff training. KLM produced an impressive body of evidence to show that its crew was highly experienced and would have been able to deal effectively with the crisis were it not for the stewards and stewardesses being overcome by fumes, and the near-three-hour delay in freezing waters and pitch dark. This was countered by accusations that the crew did not even have available to them elementary equipment such as flash-lights.

Dick McGonigal, a wily advocate, made much play of the fact that, despite concerns expressed by a Customs Officer at the Airport about the take-off, and flares having been set off by the crew, the rescue operation did not commence for three vital hours. He also played on the fact that an airport official had wrongly identified the aircraft, thus erroneously persuading his colleagues that Flight 633X was on course.

Mr Justice Teevan delivered the findings of the Inquiry to the Minister, with commendable speed, on 1 February 1955.[106] Although the Report of the Inquiry's findings emphasised criticisms of KLM — 'Air-crash Report points to errors by the KLM Captain' was the *Irish Times* headline — both the crew and the rescue operation were criticised. The Inquiry found that the Captain had failed to interpret properly certain instrument indications and had failed to maintain sufficient climb to allow him to deal with unexpected occurrences. The delay in the rescue was criticised, particularly the failure of the airport to realise, or even suspect, that the aircraft was in trouble. The Inquiry made a number of far-reaching recommendations which were quickly implemented at Shannon and far beyond. A spokesman for KLM welcomed the Report, stating that its recommendations and conclusions 'might contribute to the development and safety of civil aviation'.

A Literary Libel Action

Arthur's interest in literature meant that he particularly relished representing distinguished literary figures. He advised Oliver St John Gogarty in the celebrated libel action taken against him in 1937 by Henry Morris Sinclair, who complained that references in Gogarty's *As I was going down*

Sackville Street to an old usurer who sought sexual gratification
from enticing young girls into his office, were references to
his late grandfather, and therefore that he had been
identified and defamed as one of the grandsons who,
according to the book, had adopted their grandfather's
disgusting habits.[107] Arthur had previously advised Gogarty in
1923 when his home at Renvyle, Co. Galway, was burnt down
by the anti-Treaty forces.

The Sinclair libel case was sensational, attracting enormous
crowds each day who witnessed theatre of the highest calibre.
Sinclair's solicitors, Messrs Reddin and Reddin, retained the
services of Albert Wood KC, Joseph McCarthy KC and Ernest
Wood. This formidable team of forensic jousters was ably
matched by Arthur's choice of J.M. FitzGerald KC, Ralph
Brereton Barry KC and Oliver D. Gogarty, the defendant's
son.

No quarter was given on either side. Albert Wood accused
Gogarty of having pursued Sinclair 'with a savagery and
ghoulishness which could only fit in with the aberrations of
an amoral mind in a pot-boiling scurrility...' J.M. FitzGerald
attacked Samuel Beckett, who was not yet established as a
leading writer and who gave evidence on Sinclair's behalf, as
'a bawd and blasphemer from Paris'. Mr Justice O'Byrne
dramatically threatened to withdraw the case from the jury as
the plaintiff had failed to prove that Gogarty had written and
published the offending words, forcing Albert Wood to take
the highly unusual step of calling the defendant as a witness
for the plaintiff. The jury eventually found in favour of
Sinclair and awarded him the not insubstantial amount of
£900 damages plus costs. It was later suggested by a member
of the jury that Gogarty had been made to pay not so much
for what he had said about Sinclair but for separate insults he
had directed at Eamon de Valera.

Arthur and G.B.S.

Nine years later, in 1946, Arthur was given the opportunity to
represent an even larger name in Irish literature, in much
happier circumstances, when there arrived on the scene one
of the most colourful characters he had ever encountered.

His name was Gabriel Pascal. A Hungarian film director by profession (Pascal was not his real name), his main claim to fame was that he had persuaded the ninety-year-old George Bernard Shaw to allow him to make film versions of some of his plays. While Shaw was always dubious about Pascal he was, like virtually everyone else who ever met him, captivated by his charm and his undoubted genius as a film director. In truth, Pascal was something of a rogue, but a likeable one at that. The occasional likeable rogue was exactly what Arthur needed to take his mind off the more mundane fare of commercial contracts and business deals.

Pascal's mission in Ireland was to raise money to film Shaw's *St Joan*. The huge success of his 1935 version of *Pygmalion* (which won an Oscar) was overshadowed by the failure of his 1945 version of *Caesar and Cleopatra* which ran hugely over budget and over time, leading to Pascal being censured by the General Council of the Association of Cine-Technicians which ruled that he could work again in a British studio only under severe restriction. In Hollywood, Arthur Rank also turned his back on Pascal.

Unpopular in Britain and unwanted in Hollywood, Pascal hit upon the idea of a studio in Ireland where the plays of one of its most distinguished sons could be filmed for posterity. His timing could not have been more perfect. Throughout the late 1930s and early 1940s several proposals were made to the Department of Industry and Commerce for the creation of an Irish film industry. In 1938 the Taoiseach, Eamon de Valera, established an inquiry into cinema in Ireland. The report of this inquiry which was furnished to Sean Lemass as Minister for Industry and Commerce in 1943 fell short of the ambitious plans which Lemass had for a film industry. He later made much more elaborate proposals to Government which also ultimately failed.[108]

Pascal, on arriving in Ireland, went straight to the top. He showed *Caesar and Cleopatra* to de Valera who was reportedly enchanted by the film. The seed sown, Pascal retained Arthur's services to prepare a briefing document for consideration by de Valera and Lemass. The document entitled: 'Preliminary Heads by Way of Observations as to the Proposed Foundation of an Irish National Picture Industry' was sent by Pascal to de Valera on 30 August 1946, with a letter in which he also informed the Taoiseach that Arthur was making enquiries in relation to the acquisition of a suitable premises for the new studio.[109]

Pascal's next objective was to obtain the support of as many influential Irish people as possible. His first disciples apart from Arthur were Frank Dermody, an Irish-language theatre director and actor, and Fr Cormac OFM who apparently became involved on the recommendation of Archbishop McQuaid of Dublin. What Pascal badly needed was capital. The prospect of achieving the agreed target of £250,000 was greatly enhanced when he obtained the support of two men from opposite ends of the Irish political spectrum, namely Dan Breen, former freedom fighter and now Fianna Fáil TD, and Joe McGrath, former Cumann Na nGaedheal Minister and now Hospital Sweepstakes millionaire. It was certainly a motley crew. Pascal's wife Valerie (whom he met and married during the time of his Irish escapade) recalled meeting Arthur 'the attorney, a thin man with reddish hair', Dan Breen 'an Irish national hero who had led a flying column of young Irishmen from Tipperary against the British in Ireland's War of Independence' and an unnamed 'Grecoesque Franciscan monk', presumably Fr Cormac.[110]

Pascal insisted that the project be pursued at a frantic pace. This was essential not merely to retain Irish interest but also to underpin his relationship with the ever suspicious Shaw. He set up shop in Arthur's offices for long periods of time and stayed at Carraig Breac on many occasions. His artistic exuberance, flirtatious manner and his exotic choice of assistant in Emilia Buoncore brought a little touch of Hollywood to Stephen's Green. He even suggested to one of the apprentices that she might like to star in the film!

Arthur arranged for the formation of a company entitled Irish Productions Limited which later changed its name to Irish Screen Art Limited. The directors of the company were Arthur, Pascal, Breen, McGrath and two others introduced by Arthur: Eustace Shott, a partner in Craig Gardner and Johnny Robinson, an architect and close friend of Arthur who was given the job of vetting suitable premises. Pascal originally had loftier notions for the company's name. These were vetoed by Shaw for a reason explained by him in a letter to de Valera of 11 October 1946:

> My Dear Taoiseach,
>
> Just a line about Pascal. He proposes that his project should be called 'PascalPictures' or some variation of that.
>
> I have reminded him that the name of a living man must not be attached to a permanent institution, as you can never be sure that he will not be hanged. Parnell, though he was not hanged, was a case in point.[111]

Arthur made certain not to miss out on the opportunity to meet with Shaw and visited him at Ayot St Lawrence on at least two occasions. He had been a fan for many years. In May 1913 he had gone with his cousin Dora to see a production of Shaw's *The Devil's Disciple* at the Gaiety Theatre. He relished his meetings with Shaw although the subsequent correspondence would suggest that a considerable amount of their time was taken up with discussing the implications for Irish Screen Art of the provisions of the Control of Manufacturers Acts, in stark contrast to the conversations which Shaw had with Dan Breen on how he (Shaw) had been involved in attempts to save Sir Roger Casement. Such was the enthusiasm for the venture that, almost inevitably, its existence was leaked to the newspapers. *The Sunday Express* in London broke the story in May 1947. Shaw was furious and, according to Valerie Pascal, 'raged like a Gaelic god'.[112]

Despite an assurance from Arthur to de Valera that the money was secure, this was far from the case. Arthur's and Pascal's fundraising efforts in Ireland did not raise enough money for the production of *St Joan,* never mind the building and equipping of an Irish film studio. Pascal pleaded with Lemass for State subvention but the Government at its meeting on 23 May 1947 decided 'that the project was one in which the State would not be justified in putting up the money required by Mr Pascal for the proposed company.'[113] An extremely disappointed Shaw wrote to de Valera on 3 June, notifying him that the project was finished.

Immediately on receipt of Shaw's letter, de Valera made contact with Arthur and with Johnny Robinson to see if anything could be done. In later years, Arthur loved to recount what happened when de Valera telephoned. He was at his desk one evening when the telephone rang. When he answered, a voice said: 'Eamon de Valera here.' Assuming it to be a practical joke on the part of one of his friends Arthur replied: 'Indeed, I'm sure you are,' and put the phone down. A few seconds later an amused Taoiseach phoned again and said: 'Mr Cox, this really is Eamon de Valera.' Having got over his faux pas, Arthur again assured de Valera that he was confident that the necessary money could be raised. On 9 June 1947 de Valera replied to Shaw's letter stating:

> Apparently some of the people here regarded the proposal as highly speculative and were afraid to risk their savings in it to the amount required. The State, on the other hand, could hardly engage in a project of this sort, although before this project was mooted at all we were considering the provision of a National studio, with adjoined facilities, to be rented out to the producing companies.

> Since I received your letter I have spoken to Cox and to Robinson. They are also very keen on it and are excellent businessmen with very wide connections. Cox is, I understand, writing to you himself and will no doubt put his ideas before you. As for McGrath, there seems to be some difficulty in his case but if anyone can iron out that, I am sure Cox and Robinson will do it.[114]

Dan Breen now travelled to see Shaw and implored him to give the project more time. Pascal, meantime, was in Italy making arrangements for the production there of *Androcles and the Lion.* Shaw agreed to Breen's request and Arthur set about drafting an agreement for signature by Shaw which would give Irish Screen Art the right to film his plays. The agreement was finally signed by Shaw on 8 September 1947 and two weeks later Shaw issued a press release enthusiastically endorsing the plan:

> I have had in mind for a long time the fitness of Ireland as a field for film industry. The climate, the scenery, the dramatic aptitudes of the people, all point that way. The present domination of Hollywood over the enormous influence of screen pictures on the mind of the world is to

me deplorable: it is creating a barbarous sock-in-the-jaw morality on the whole world from which Ireland must be rescued. Having already municipalized my Irish landed property, I am ready to give Ireland the first call on my valuable film rights.[115]

While Arthur, Pascal and Breen now had Shaw's signature on the agreement and his public endorsement of the project, the truth was that despite their best efforts they had failed to secure the necessary finance. They avoided bringing this to Shaw's attention until the last possible moment. By November 1947 it was clear that there was no prospect of adequate finance being raised. Shaw, on receiving a copy of Board Minutes of Irish Screen Art became extremely annoyed and, in typical fashion, flashed off letters to Pascal, de Valera, Breen and to Arthur. His letter to Breen was the most animated:

Dear Dan,

Get all this sentimental rubbish out of your blessed old noodle; I have no feeling in business. You can't humbug me; and it grieves me that you have humbugged yourself to the tune of £1,000.

I have given you time to do your damnedest to raise Irish capital... The simplest and perhaps the honestest thing for the S.A. Limited would be to wind up and pocket its losses, but after the company has been advertised as it has been, its failure would be a failure for Ireland. What is the available alternative? First to get rid of me and Pascal. The Protestant capitalists will not back me because I am on talking terms with you, and do not believe that you will go to hell when you die. The clergy, now that they know that I will not write up the Saints for them, will not back a notorious Free Thinker. The Catholic laity will not back a bloody Protestant. The capitalists who have no religion and no politics except money-making rule me out as a highbrow in whom there is no money. All of them object to Pascal because he is a foreigner who throws away millions as if they were three penny bits. So out we go with our contracts torn up.[116]

His letter to Arthur also betrayed his deep disappointment. Arthur's reply in turn showed a deep personal hurt. He was extremely defensive of his role and that of his colleagues in the project, indeed unduly defensive in response to what should have been seen as an inevitable reaction from Shaw. Having outlined in great detail his involvement with the project, Arthur went on:

> I am only an obscure Irish attorney. I hope — despite what you say — that I am not really a highbrow. But Dan Breen's name is a good one, and so are those of Mr McGrath, Mr Shott and Mr Robinson. None of them would have promised more than they could perform.

> It was therefore a very great and unexpected shock to us to receive your letter, which places us in what we honestly, not merely believe, but know to be a false light.

> We undertook this burden — and it was a real burden to busy men — not with a view to personal profit, but, because we did not want you, the greatest Irishman since St Patrick (who was not an Irishman at all) to think that Ireland wholly failed to respond when you made your generous call. It was a call the Irish Government could not answer — although we know it would gladly have done so in less austere times — but we did not wish that you should go unanswered. It was a just cause of pride to us to be permitted, however humbly, to share a little in the illumination of your genius. It is therefore a sorrow to us that the end should have come just at the moment, when after a good deal of anxiety, much work, and the expenditure of a few thousand, we had in fact done what we had promised.

> To us frankly, it is a great sorrow that matters should have so ended. It is however reasonable to think from your letter that you wish it to be so and as we have done from the start we accept your Wish as our Law. But we do not like you to think we have been false or even foolish. It only remains to say that all of us, in parting, wish God speed to you, Mr Pascal, and to Androcles.[117]

Arthur's letter, with its mixture of robust defence and exaggerated courtesy, caused Shaw to reply that there was no misunderstanding nor unfriendliness on his side and that he was gratefully conscious of the heroic efforts made by Arthur and Dan Breen to raise capital on the strength of his reputation. The letter of 12 December 1947 from George Bernard Shaw to Arthur Cox was the last piece of correspondence in what had been an exciting but ultimately fruitless venture. Arthur's interest in the film business was revived in the 1950s when he advised John Huston on his early forays into Irish film-making.

One commentator has suggested that the Pascal project failed 'because Cox's sensitive Catholic antennae had picked up the rumour that Pope Pius XII's advisers were not happy about having their Church's burning of a Saint sympathetically explained and defended to cinema audiences by an Irish lapsed Protestant.'[118] While this explanation is intriguing, it would seem that the true cause was the more banal one of lack of finance. It was another decade before Ireland's first and only permanent film studio was built. Ironically, one of the driving forces behind that venture was Emmet Dalton, yet another figure from the War of Independence.

8

The Hinge of Fate

IN August 1942 a very distinguished visitor arrived to a caravan in Egypt to demand explanations from war-weary soldiers. He left unimpressed. Nine years later one of the soldiers went into Hodges Figgis in Dublin and bought two copies of the distinguished visitor's recently published memoirs. On 15 October 1953 Arthur received a letter from Messrs Nicholl Manisty & Co., Solicitors, of London asking if he would act in Ireland for their client, the Rt Hon. Sir Winston L.S. Churchill, KG,OM,CH,DL,MP, who was being threatened with libel proceedings in Ireland by Brigadier Eric Dorman-O'Gowan (formerly Dorman-Smith) in respect of certain passages in Volume IV of Churchill's *The Second World War* which was entitled *The Hinge of Fate*.

Arthur replied immediately saying he would be 'most highly honoured to act'. He obtained permission to retain the services of two leading Senior Counsel and one Junior Counsel, which was usual if a major libel action was on the horizon. Niall McLaughlin was asked to retain the services of Arthur's old friend John A. Costello SC along with James McGuire SC and Felix Sherry. Arthur's obvious pleasure at being asked to act for such an illustrious client allowed his normally taciturn self to be replaced by unconcealed enthusiasm leading him to admit in his note to Niall McLaughlin 'I am very excited about this case!'[119]

The alleged libel arose in Chapters 26 and 29 of Churchill's book, which dealt with his visit as Prime Minister to Cairo in August 1942. At the time of his visit, the High Command in the Middle East was led by General Auchinleck. The Deputy Chief of the General Staff was Major General Dorman-Smith.

Churchill's visit to Cairo was prompted by rumours he had heard of problems in the desert army and suggestions that Auchinleck had lost the confidence of his men. He was clearly alarmed by the defeat at Gazala on 15 June followed five days later by the loss of Tobruk. The meeting in the tent and Churchill's other discussions with Auchinleck and Dorman-Smith did little to assuage his concerns. He decided that 'drastic and immediate change' was needed. On 8 August, two days after his visit, Dorman-Smith was removed from his position as Deputy Chief of the General Staff. His removal was described in *The Hinge of Fate* as having been required by 'the gravity and urgency of the situation'. Later in the book Churchill wrote:

I am sure we were heading for disaster under the former regime. The Army was reduced to bits and pieces and oppressed by a sense of bafflement and uncertainty. Apparently it was intended in face of heavy attack to retire Eastwards to the Delta. Many were looking over their shoulders to make sure of their seat in the lorry, and no plan of battle or dominating willpower had reached the Units.

Eric Dorman-Smith was born near Cootehill, Co. Cavan on 24 July 1895. He fought in both World Wars, his military career ending in 1944 in less than happy circumstances. He returned to Cavan to the family estate at Bellamont, where he led a life increasingly isolated from his former colleagues and from the country for which he had fought valiantly on two occasions. In 1949 he changed his name to Dorman-O'Gowan (O'Gowan being an Irish version of Smith). He contested elections unsuccessfully on both sides of the Irish border, campaigned vigorously against partition and, as Arthur politely described it, 'interested himself in the Irish national movement'.

Shortly after purchasing his copies of Churchill's book, Dorman-O'Gowan consulted his cousin, Philip Smith, who practised as a solicitor in Cavan under the title Louis C.P. Smith & Co. Philip Smith was an eminent and well respected member of his profession who, by chance, was a good friend of Arthur. He had fought in the First World War, escaping from a German prison only to be recaptured at the Dutch border. On 1 May 1953 Smith wrote to Churchill alleging that passages in his book had the effect of branding Dorman-O'Gowan as 'incompetent and perhaps worse'. He pointed out that Dorman-O'Gowan was not appointed Deputy Chief of Staff until 16 June and took no official part in operations until 25 June, so that he could not have been responsible for the setbacks at Gazala or Tobruk. The letter was a spirited defence of Dorman-O'Gowan and of Auchinleck, quoting no less a person than Rommel as having paid generous tribute to their military achievements.

Far from being a dispirited retreat, the move to El Alamein had forced Rommel to abandon his own strategy to assist the Italians who were now under pressure. 'The one thing that mattered to (Auchinleck)', Rommel recorded later, 'was to halt our advance, and that unfortunately he had done.'[120] Mussolini likewise saw this 'retreat' as a turning point: 'I told (Hitler) that we had lost the initiative ... and that a nation which had lost the initiative had lost the war.'[121]

Philip Smith left Churchill in no doubt as to how strongly his client felt: 'Your history... has spread the story of incompetence to the ends of the earth. It has caused him untold pain and humiliation. To many soldiers all over the world he is branded as a failure and named by a famous statesman as being responsible for their suffering. To many parents and wives he is labelled as the cause of the death of those whom they have lost.'

Between May and October 1953, Smith was involved in protracted correspondence with Nicholl Manisty & Co. for Churchill, and another London firm of solicitors Oswald Hickson Collier & Co. who were retained by Cassells, the publishers of the book. Churchill refused to accept that his words led to the conclusions of which Dorman-Smith complained and declined to modify his comments in any way. On 2 October, Smith confirmed that his client intended to commence proceedings in Ireland and called on Churchill's London solicitors to nominate Irish solicitors to accept service of proceedings. This, in turn, led to Arthur receiving his instructions.

As well as Nicholl Manisty & Co. in London and now Arthur Cox & Co. in Dublin, Churchill was also receiving advice, albeit on an informal basis, from another eminent legal source. The leader of the English Bar at the time was the former Labour Attorney General, Sir Hartley Shawcross (now Lord Shawcross). Shawcross had achieved international acclaim as chief British prosecutor at the Nuremberg trials. Although on opposite sides in the House of Commons, the two men became friends and Churchill frequently sought Shawcross's advice on matters — not always legal matters — after Labour's defeat in the 1951 election which returned the eighty-year-old Churchill to power.

Arthur did not allow his enthusiasm for the case to be dampened by the arrival on his home patch of such a noted foreign lawyer, nor did he appear to resent the unorthodox but pivotal role played by Shawcross in the unfolding drama. He would later jokingly complain that Shawcross had ruined everything by settling a case which would have enthralled the Irish public if it had been allowed to come to Court. If Churchill wanted Shawcross as lead player, then Arthur was willing to assume the role of conductor of the legal orchestra.

Arthur arranged a series of meetings at his office on St Stephen's Green on Saturday, 24 October 1953. Mr Burrows of Nicholl Manisty & Co. arrived the previous evening and dined with Arthur at the Stephen's Green Club where he was filled in on the Irish scene and the risks inherent in Churchill having to face an Irish jury. Shawcross flew to Dublin the following morning and was met at the airport by Arthur. His arrival attracted the attention of the media. A reporter at the airport enquired of Arthur whether his guest was in Dublin in relation to an action being taken by the British Turf Club against an Irish trainer. 'World-famed lawyer's air dash to Dublin', reported the following day's *Sunday Press*. The newspapers bombarded Arthur and his Counsel with questions on the reason for Shawcross's visit. Happily for those at the centre of the case, *The Irish Times* on Monday 26 October led the other papers on a merry dance by exclusively revealing that 'Sir Hartley's visit was concerned with the forthcoming legal action in Britain for the return of the remains of Sir Roger Casement.'[122] Arthur faithfully forwarded copies of all newspaper cuttings to Burrows, remarking that in their excitement over Shawcross's believed involvement in the Casement matter 'some people seem to think that I have the body of Sir Roger concealed somewhere in my office.' Within a few days the newspapers knew the true reason for Shawcross's visit.

At noon, Arthur, Burrows and Shawcross met with Dorman-O'Gowan, Philip Smith and his Counsel, Sir John Esmonde SC. The formal gloomy office in 42 St Stephen's Green can rarely have housed such a distinguished gathering. The meeting continued into the afternoon, through a break for a quick lunch in the Shelbourne Hotel. The atmosphere was tense. A lot of the discussion took place between Dorman-O'Gowan and Shawcross alone. Shawcross was left in no doubt of how gravely Dorman-O'Gowan viewed the situation and of his intent to pursue the matter. He quickly formed the view that it was imperative that an amicable solution be found. A British Prime Minister being forced to appear in a foreign Court was unseemly. Winston Churchill, who eight years earlier had launched an extraordinary tirade against Ireland's neutrality in World War II, having to face an Irish jury was unthinkable. The British army would be forced to take opposite sides in an Irish Court: Dorman-O'Gowan and Auchinleck on one side, Alexander and Montgomery on the other.

Above all these considerations was the risk to Churchill's health if he was forced to appear in Court. Shawcross knew that his friend was very unwell; the risk of him collapsing under the strain of a Court appearance was very real. He laboured this aspect with Dorman-O'Gowan, who he rightly perceived as not being vindictive but rather determined to right what he saw as the injustice done to Auchinleck more than to himself. Arthur accompanied Shawcross to the airport that evening. They were agreed that Churchill should, at the very least, agree to modify the offending text. The difficulty faced by Shawcross was to persuade Churchill to focus on this relatively trivial matter long enough to recognise the dangers inherent in adopting an unyielding approach.

Dorman-O'Gowan enlisted the help of the distinguished military historian, Captain Basil Liddell Hart, to advise on the accuracy of his version of the events of 1942. At the end of November, Philip Smith wrote to Arthur setting out the terms on which Dorman-O'Gowan would be willing to abandon his action. He pointed out that a trial would not only allow his client to vindicate his reputation but would also afford him the opportunity to have investigated in public the mystery surrounding the sudden ending of his military career. Of the many points which Shawcross had made at the meeting, the one which Smith identified as appealing to Dorman-O'Gowan was that Churchill was 'advanced in years and bearing great burdens'. For that reason alone Dorman-O'Gowan was willing to settle on the basis that a lengthy addendum be inserted as a footnote at the end of the offending page. His decision was also clearly influenced by the lack of enthusiasm shown by Auchinleck who found the idea of an action against Churchill 'distasteful'.

Arthur sought to lessen the effect of the suggested footnote by having it inserted as an Appendix which could be 'buried' among the other Appendices 'without suggesting to the reader that there was any special reason for its inclusion'. When Philip Smith showed no interest in this suggestion, Arthur then suggested a very short footnote. Churchill drafted a six-line factual footnote, Dorman-O'Gowan added to it and agreement was reached on its text, which read:

> The reference to the Officers whose names figure in this list are factual only and are not to be taken as imputing any personal blame to individuals. These were the principal changes in commands and staff at the time when General Auchinleck was replaced by General Alexander.

> Major General Dorman-Smith only became Deputy Chief of Staff on 16th June 1942. He thus bears no responsibility for the fall of Tobruk or the defeat at Gazala. From 25th June to 4th August he acted as General Auchinleck's Operations Officer at headquarters Eighth Army during the operation described in Chapter 24. My appreciation in that Chapter of the handling of the Eighth Army is supported by Rommel's remarkable tribute.

While the agreed footnote resolved the issue in respect of Dorman-O'Gowan's removal as Deputy Chief, there remained in Dorman-O'Gowan's view the separate calumny of the 'retreat to the Delta' passage, along with the question of costs. Churchill was adamant that, since the passage did not refer to Dorman-O'Gowan by name, no amendment was required.

It was agreed that the best hope of an amicable settlement lay in a further meeting between Dorman-O'Gowan and Shawcross. On Sunday 3 May 1954 Sir Hartley Shawcross once more flew to Dublin. His arrival at 4.20 pm went unnoticed by the media. The venue for the meeting was Carraig Breac. Philip Smith, Sir John Esmonde and their client arrived at 4.30 pm. Liddell Hart, who was supposed to accompany Dorman-O'Gowan, had to cancel his visit at short notice. Arthur reported that the atmosphere was friendly, much more friendly than at the earlier meeting in his office. This was no doubt influenced by the tranquil setting overlooking Dublin Bay and by the hospitality shown to her guests by Brigid Cox. Shawcross's recollection of the Carraig Breac meeting is that it was again tense. He was once more left alone for some time with Dorman-O'Gowan, both of them pacing up and down the book-lined drawing room. Eventually, a modification to the earlier footnote was agreed. Arthur again sought to dilute its effect by recommending to Churchill that a number of other new footnotes should appear in the new edition, 'so that this footnote will not stand out too prominently'.

The matter was now settled subject to the question of costs. Arthur emphatically argued that for Churchill to concede on costs was to admit some liability and was 'impossible'. In the end, the publishers made a contribution to Dorman-O'Gowan's costs privately, so that Churchill could always deny that costs had been paid.

Shawcross's final act was to draft a press statement which was to be released jointly by Churchill and Dorman-O'Gowan. The latter, however, spoke to the press before the press release, provoking headlines on 2 July: 'Irish Ex-General's Legal Victory over Churchill' in *The Irish Times* and 'Libel in Churchill Memoirs' in the *Irish Press*. Arthur issued a strong denial that the implications of the newspaper reports were acceptable. His statement received wide coverage on 3 July.

There now remained only the question of Arthur's costs. Writing in November 1954 to Nicholl Manisty & Co. Arthur suggested a fee of 300 guineas plus expenses but did not press for payment: 'This was, however, no ordinary client, and the writer would have been very honoured and overjoyed if he had been asked to act in the case for nothing... acting for him even in what to him was of no great consequence was a very great honour in itself and, as we have said, we should be just as happy if there were no fee at all. If it were possible we should like Sir Winston to know — as we are sure he does — that in Ireland he has as many admirers as in any other country, and that is saying much.'

In the end, Churchill reimbursed Arthur for his out of pocket expenses which came to £46.15.3. He declared himself 'grateful and touched' by Arthur's gesture in waiving his fee and sent, through the Irish Embassy in London, a signed copy of his *Life of Marlborough* 'in token appreciation for all the help and consideration you have shown me'. Arthur was delighted to receive the books which comprised two volumes beautifully bound in red leather and gilt-edged which he 'treasured as something infinitely more valuable than any payment could have been'. In deciding to waive his fees, Arthur could not resist an opportunity to be seen to make the grand gesture. 'We are not sure' he wrote to Nicholl Manisty & Co. on 22 November 1954, 'whether Aesop mentioned it in his Fables, but we think that he might have made reference to the occasion on which the mouse made a small birthday present to the lion on his 80th birthday. Aesop did not mention whether the mouse was an Irish one.'

The Churchill/Dorman-O'Gowan saga was resurrected temporarily in 1956 and later in 1959 when Philip Smith justifiably complained that, years after the settlement, copies of *The Hinge of Fate* still did not carry the agreed footnote. This was eventually resolved. The last letter on Arthur's file was typical of his discretion. It was to Nicholl Manisty & Co. on 11 March 1959 and after referring to an earlier letter read simply: 'The writer happened to meet with Mr Philip Smith in his

Club a few days ago. Mr Smith did not then refer to this case and, of course, the writer did not.'

The Churchill case contained all the ingredients so loved by Arthur — a high profile client, political intrigue and a requirement for the utmost secrecy. His only regret — apart from jokingly lamenting that it never came to Court — was that he did not get to meet Churchill. On several occasions he offered to 'run over to London' to speak with Nicholl Manisty & Co. Lord Shawcross's most vivid memory of Arthur, apart from the fact that he was 'agreeable, sensible and nice',[123] is of him complaining that he was not being afforded the opportunity to meet his client. Arthur would have been less than human if he had not wished to meet Churchill. Perhaps his interest in meeting Churchill was even greater than that of someone who simply wished to shake hands with a famous man. Perhaps he wished to meet the man who had described his close friend Kevin O'Higgins — his wife's first husband — as 'a figure from the antique cast in bronze'.[124] That tribute alone would have been enough to endear Winston Churchill to Arthur Cox.

9

Public Life

For the most part Arthur remained aloof from the issues facing his profession, although if required to do so he always stoutly defended its integrity and its independence. In his Inaugural Address as Auditor of the Solicitors Apprentices' Debating Society delivered on 29 October 1913 on the topic of 'The Lawyer in Literature' he had complained about the manner in which lawyers had been harshly treated in literature through the centuries. Although not yet a member of the profession, he delivered an eloquent and forceful defence of the role of lawyers: 'Grub Street has every right to object to the disturbance of its quiet walks by the impious tread of the writ-server. That Grub Street cannot pay its debts does not entitle it to vilify for centuries an honourable profession.'[125]

The solicitors' profession in Ireland is self-regulated and extremely protective of its independence. Its professional body is the Incorporated Law Society of Ireland which is charged with the training, disciplining and regulating of the profession as well as acting as the body entrusted with protecting the interests of its members and their clients. The controlling body of the Incorporated Law Society is its Council consisting of members of the profession elected each year by their professional peers.

Arthur was persuaded to seek election to the Council in 1941. By this time, his reputation in the profession was without equal. He secured third place in the election at his first attempt, getting 347 votes — just 1 vote less than Eugene F. Collins in second place, and 13 votes behind J. Travers Wolfe who topped the poll. The following year Arthur replaced Travers Wolfe at the head of the poll. For the remainder of his time on the Council, Arthur's vote remained strong, his only serious contender for first place being Henry St John Blake.[126]

The highest honour a profession can bestow on one of its members is to elect him or her as head of its professional body. The tradition in the Incorporated Law Society is that members of the Council will, if they continue to be re-elected, become a Vice-President and later President of the Society.

The practice is that each Council member who wishes to serve as President will be elected, in turn, by the Council to the post. When Arthur joined the Council a new member could expect to become President within about ten years. The thirty-one members elected to Council each year usually included a number of Past Presidents who remained eligible for election to the Council. There were also members who, for various reasons, chose not to seek election as President. Not least among these were financial considerations. Presidents at the time received relatively modest subvention from the Society with the result that only Council members with thriving practices could afford the considerable expense involved. One tradition which continued until the late 1950s was that the President was expected to host a lavish dinner for the entire Council at which the best of food, wine and entertainment was provided.

Arthur became a Vice-President of the Incorporated Law Society in 1943. The Council chose him as their President for the session 1951/52. Becoming President of the Incorporated Law Society is an honour for each person fortunate enough to hold that office. The year 1952 was particularly important in the Society's history. The seed which grew to become the present Society was planted in 1791 with the formation of the Law Club of Ireland. The Law Society of Ireland was founded in 1830. The direct roots of the present Society are traced to 1841 when the Society of the Attorneys and Solicitors of Ireland was formed. The Society received its Charter of Incorporation in 1852, which created the Incorporated Society of the Attorneys and Solicitors of Ireland as 'a body political and corporate with perpetual succession and a common seal'.[127]

The war being waged in Europe in 1941 had made it impractical and inappropriate for the Society to mark the centenary of its formation. Instead, it was decided that the centenary of its Charter should be celebrated in style. The preparations for the centenary celebrations of 1952 began years earlier under the guidance of the Society's Secretary, Eric Plunkett. Arthur's year as President was dominated by those celebrations. His shy diffident nature, his lack of enthusiasm for all forms of socialising, and his single-minded dedication to his work and his clients did not lend themselves to the public role on which he was now obliged to embark. He had, of course, a marvellous ally and source of encouragement in his wife. Despite his reservations, Arthur threw himself with enthusiasm into the role, conscious of the importance to his profession of the centenary celebrations.

The formal opening of the celebrations was a reception hosted by Arthur and Brigid in the Great Hall of the Four Courts and the Society's Library on 27 May 1952. The President of Ireland Sean T. O Ceallaigh and his wife entertained about fourteen hundred guests at a Garden Party at Aras an Uachtarain. Arthur and Brigid joined the President and Mrs O Ceallaigh in welcoming the guests. The evening of 28 May saw the climax of the official celebrations at the Charter Centenary Dinner held at the Gresham Hotel.

The toast to the Society was proposed by Dr Michael Tierney, President of University College, Dublin. Arthur and Dr Tierney had known each other for many years. Two years earlier, Arthur had acted for Tierney in an action taken against him by a student named Hackett who claimed that Tierney had slandered him in front of two other University officials by alleging that the student had obtained a grant by false pretences. To the dismay of many, the jury found in favour of the student and awarded him £750 damages together with costs. Arthur advised strongly that Tierney should appeal the decision and, ultimately, the appeal was successful.

Dr Tierney, having remarked that the Incorporated Law Society shared its centenary with University College, informed his audience that he had joined UCD as a student in 1911, the year Arthur Cox was elected as Auditor of the

L & H. (In fact, Arthur was not elected until 1912). He went on to say that Arthur 'was one of the best Auditors the Society has ever had, and his year of office is still remembered even by the short-lived student generations. Mr Cox is one of those rare men who, even in their youth, set an example which is looked back to by those who have come after them.'[128]

Arthur's reply on behalf of the Society was a mixture of dignified formality and understated wit. Having thanked his guests and the proposer of the toast, he paid tribute to some of the distinguished former members of the profession, in particular Pat Hogan whom he described as his 'dearest friend'. He then reflected on the role of his own profession through the following anecdote:

> I understand that in the course of the Spanish Civil War whenever the Reds entered a village, their first step was to take out the priest, the mayor and the solicitor to shoot them and that when the Franco forces entered they in turn took out the leader of the trade union and the solicitor and shot them. I think that unanimity was no mere tribute. I think it does show the place the solicitor plays in the community — what the lawyer stands for as Dr Tierney said. He stands for the common liberty and the rights of the ordinary human being which today are menaced in so many ways and in many lands. I think that the legal profession in this country, both barristers and solicitors, may fairly claim that in the troubled years which this country went through at one time, they stood for the liberty and fundamental rights of the people of this country and I believe that they will always continue so to stand.

Apart from the formal celebrations held in May 1952, Arthur was obliged to attend numerous function throughout the country and abroad. Traditionally, each local Bar Association invites the President and his wife to attend its annual dinner, giving the local solicitors an opportunity to discuss with the President the issues most affecting them in their practice. Arthur attended relatively few of these functions, sending a representative to attend on his behalf. He did travel to Donegal to hear the concerns being expressed about Northern Ireland solicitors seeking business in the Republic. He also attended the annual meetings of the Waterford Law Society and the Midlands Solicitors' Association, and was guest of the Northern Ireland Law Society in Belfast and the Scottish Law Society in Gleneagles.

Apart from day to day problems within the profession, the issues which exercised the minds of the Council members during Arthur's year as President were the perennial question of the relationship between solicitors and the Bar and the advent of the Solicitors' Bill to which Arthur would contribute in another capacity later.[129] Arthur remained a member of the Council of the Incorporated Law Society until he retired from practice in 1961. On his departure he donated to the Society a chair which had belonged to John Mitchel, lawyer and author of *Jail Journal*, and a bust of Chief Justice Malone.

The year after Arthur's Presidency, his mother died. She was ninety years of age. For the best part of ten years she was a patient in St Vincent's Hospital at 58 St Stephen's Green. Arthur visited her at least once a day during those years, strolling from his office on the same side of the Green.

Even after his mother's death, Arthur remained reluctant to sell 26 Merrion Square. Eventually, after much persuasion from Jim Beddy, he agreed to sell the house to ICC for use as its premises. The one condition Arthur attached to the sale was that he should not be obliged to attend any meetings in the house to which he remained deeply attached. Some years later, in a moment of forgetfulness, he agreed to meet a client at ICC's headquarters. Obliged to re-enter the house which brought back so many memories, Dublin's leading solicitor stood in the hallway and wept openly.

Arthur's high-profile year as President of the Incorporated Law Society led to public recognition of the talents which he had displayed over the previous three decades in his own intensely private manner on behalf of his clients and, directly and indirectly, on behalf of successive Governments. In 1951 he was appointed to the Company Law Reform Committee. He later became its Chairman and played a significant role in the preparation of the Committee's Report which was presented to the Government in 1958. The Cox Report as it is more widely known, was the first comprehensive review of Irish Company Law since independence and was given public expression in the Companies Act, 1963.[130] On 8 July 1952 he joined his late father on the list of people recognised by the National University of Ireland through the conferring of an Honorary Degree, the LL.D.

In the summer of 1954 Arthur received a call from his old friend John A. Costello, whose services as a Senior Counsel Arthur had retained on many occasions, most recently on behalf of Winston Churchill. Costello had been Attorney General from 1926 to 1932 and became a TD in 1933. His first fifteen years in the Dáil were spent in opposition. This allowed him to concentrate on his substantial practice at the Bar. In the General Election of 1948 Fine Gael fared very badly, a proliferation of small parties having split the anti-Fianna Fáil vote. So determined was the opposition, fragmented and all as it was, to oust de Valera that an Inter-Party Government comprising Fine Gael (led by Richard Mulcahy), Labour (led by William Norton), Clann na Poblachta (led by Sean McBride), Clann na Talmhan (led by Joseph Blowick), National Labour (led by James Everett), and the former Fine Gael TD James Dillon, then an Independent, was eventually formed with the Ministerial spoils of war shared between them on an equitable basis.

Fine Gael did not merely snatch survival from the jaws of oblivion, but as the largest party in the new Government became entitled to nominate its leader as Taoiseach. This caused a problem. Mulcahy's role as Minister for Defence and Commander-in-Chief during the Civil War made him totally unacceptable to McBride's new republican party and not greatly favoured by the Labour Party either. Mulcahy quickly realised that his nomination to the post of Taoiseach would be divisive and magnanimously agreed to allow another member of his party be chosen for the position, although he remained leader of Fine Gael until 1959.

The torch passed to John A. Costello, acceptable to his fellow barrister Sean McBride and to the Labour Party as someone not burdened with the baggage of Civil War division. Costello was at first 'appalled at the idea' and consulted with many friends and colleagues on the advisability of accepting the position. As other college contemporaries had done in the past, it was to Arthur that Costello finally turned. In a memorandum written by Costello some time later, he outlined the process by which he became Taoiseach as follows:

> I also determined to consult my old friend, Mr Arthur Cox, and arranged to meet him at 5 o'clock on Sunday afternoon in his office. I attended at the office with my friends the late Mr Richard Browne and Mr Richard Rice and I put the position to Mr Cox who, after hearing all the points of view, gave it as his firm opinion that there was no way out for me but to accept nomination.[131]

Costello later elaborated on his meeting with Arthur. 'We had remained friends since our college days and were professionally associated. I valued his advice and secretly hoped he would advise me against. But he was logical. "You have been in politics for thirty years and you cannot refuse the top post. If you play with fire you must expect to get burned sometime." Had he advised against I would have been tempted to stay in the law.'[132] That night, John A. Costello consented to become Taoiseach.

The Inter-Party Government formed in 1948 fell in 1951 in the wake of the controversy over the Mother and Child Scheme. The Fianna Fáil Government elected in 1951 fell, in turn, at the General Election of 1954 and Costello returned as Taoiseach leading a second Inter-Party Government.

The 1937 Constitution allows an incoming Taoiseach to nominate eleven members to the Senate. One of those nominated by Costello in 1954 was Arthur Cox. Having eschewed all the efforts made thirty years earlier by O'Higgins and others to persuade him to enter public life, Arthur's talents were no longer to rest on the river's brim, if ever in fact they had. He was extremely pleased by the honour bestowed on him and the trust placed in him by the Taoiseach. No doubt he also relished the prospect of renewing his debating rivalry with George O'Brien. O'Brien had been a member of the Senate since 1948 when he was elected as one of the three representatives of the graduates of the National University. He remained in the Senate until 1965. James Meenan, in commenting on O'Brien's election in 1948, noted that

O'Brien confided to a friend at the time of his election his delight that at long last he had done something that Arthur Cox would have loved to do but had not done![133]

The new Senate met for the first time on 22 July 1954. Five days later Senator Arthur Cox made his maiden speech on the Final Stage of the Health Bill. It was a brief and not particularly important contribution but it set the style and tone for his later speeches — a modest and polite tone punctuated with 'It would seem to me' or 'It appears to me' often accompanied by the phrase favoured by lawyers, 'with respect', and yet betraying the incisiveness and clarity of thought for which he was renowned. In his second speech, this time on certain technical aspects of the Public Authorities (Judicial Proceedings) Bill, the introduction to his speech further developed the style: 'I support the Bill, but it occurs to me that the Minister might consider whether the technical wording might not be improved. It seems to me as a lawyer that some confusion may arise as between sub-sections (i) and (5) of Section 2 ...'[134]

Arthur's first major contribution in the Senate came in December 1954 on the Second Stage of the Solicitors' Bill. It proved enormously valuable to the profession in general and to the Incorporated Law Society in particular to have such an articulate and committed supporter involved in the process leading to the enactment of the Solicitors' Act, 1954. Two years earlier, in his reply to the toast at the Charter Centenary Dinner, Arthur had chided the then Minister for the delay in introducing the Bill: 'A surprising fact in connection with this Centenary — the Centenary of the granting by Queen Victoria of our Charter — is that she appears to have been a fast young lady because it took her fewer years from her accession to sign our Charter than it has taken our Minister not to produce our Bill.'[135]

By the time Arthur spoke for the first time on the Bill in the Senate, fifteen years had elapsed since it had been originally mooted. In his first contribution to the debate, he returned to a theme which he had taken up all those years ago in his Inaugural address to the Solicitors Apprentices' Debating Society:

The solicitor's profession is probably unique in that it is a profession which has to make itself unpleasant to a lot of people very often. A doctor enjoys the great advantage in coming in contact only with his patients, who invariably experience his kindness and help. Unfortunately for himself, the solicitor has to spend much of his time standing on the toes of other people in the interests of his client, and it is for that reason also that it is necessary to strengthen the hand of the Council of the Law Society in dealing with these cases.[136]

He defended the right of the Council of the Incorporated Law Society, as a democratically elected body, to make regulations regarding Solicitors' accounts without first having them approved by a General Meeting of the Society as was favoured by other Senators: 'I fail to see how regulations could be approved before they have been made. The Senator's proposal reminds me of the Scottish remark: "If you had seen these robes before they were made, you would bless the name of General Wade." It seems to me that the regulations must be made before they can be approved.'[137] He spoke on virtually every section of the Bill debated in the Senate, persuading his colleagues to withdraw any amendment which sought to limit the wide powers being given to the Society in respect of the disciplining of its members.

Arthur enjoyed performing on his new stage. While the Senate provided a public and yet very dignified platform from which to air his views, the many demands on his time meant that he rarely attended unless he wished to speak. As might be expected, he was at his best in dealing with Bills of a complex legal character requiring a considerable grasp of detail, such as the Factories Bill, 1954 and the Gaming and Lotteries Bill, 1955.

Arthur was always very insistent that law and order must be maintained whatever the cost. In this he was greatly influenced by the attitudes and experiences of his friends who had taken upon themselves the task of building and defending the State thirty years earlier and, in particular, by the hard line adopted by Kevin O'Higgins. Thus, in the only speech he made in the Senate which was even mildly

controversial, he opposed the abolition of capital punishment
when the matter came before the house in May 1956:

> The first duty of the State or any such organisation is to
> protect the citizens, and the first duty of this State is to
> protect the lives of those who live here. If there is any reason
> for believing that the death penalty is a deterrent, then I
> would say it should be retained, and, as I have said, I
> personally do not doubt that it is a deterrent. I am not
> sure that I agree with the point of view that seems to have
> been expressed by the previous speakers that punishment
> should be excluded. Speaking now as a Christian, I rather
> think that crime does merit punishment and that there
> should not be too much sympathy for a person who has
> been justly found to have committed a terrible crime. I
> believe personally that the death penalty is a deterrent and
> that the element of shame involved in it is also a deterrent.
> I hope and believe that I am not in any way a bloodthirsty
> person, and any little experience I have had in such cases
> has shown me the horror of them.[138]

The common thread running through many of his
speeches on issues less emotive than the security of the State
was a deep concern for the rights of the individual and, in
particular, the right of the citizen to protection from undue
State interference. He firmly supported the introduction of
the Married Women's Status Bill in 1956, declaring himself
'as anxious as everyone else to ensure that the status of women
should be both as strong and as good as that of men' and
adopting an enlightened approach to the question of
women's rights which was not fully reflected in the Act or in
legislation for many years afterwards. He expressed his views
as follows:

> I hold they should have exactly the same rights as men. But
> it is the experience of everyone who has to deal with this
> kind of case that you do get cases of a woman with property
> who has to be defended or ought to be defended against
> the attempts of her husband to get at her property.

> One very important part of a marriage ceremony is that the
> husband gives his wife the right to his property or goods.

Of course, to a large extent, in practice, that is nonsense nowadays because it does not mean that the wife gets all the husband's investments or anything like that, but it does mean that she gets very great rights in many ways to his property, to live in his house and use his things — to do all sorts of things. If the Bill were passed in its present form, it undoubtedly means that the wife can prevent her husband from interfering with any of her property. That is a very sensible and a very just thing and I fully agree with it.... [139]

During his brief three-year term in the Senate, Arthur impressed his fellow Senators. He was always clear and concise, never less than courteous. He brought to the House a wisdom born out of years of experience as a practising lawyer. His speeches were rarely inspiring but they did on occasion contain glimpses of the wry humour and insight which was so much a part of his character. His contribution to the debate on the Gaming and Lotteries Bill is an example:

Like Senator Hayes, I do not know much about public houses, but I have observed in the course of my few travels abroad that, in England, the public house does seem to be a much more pleasant sort of place than the public house here, and that very largely seems to be because it is used as a sort of club and people play games, darts and such games. I have never taken a drink, but I have been in public houses in London and elsewhere in the evening, and I must say that they present a picture which is quite different from anything one associates with an Irish public house, and that is entirely due to the fact that games are allowed there.

I support this amendment. The slot machines are a form of gambling, but a mild and popular form, and it would be strange if visitors to places like Tramore could not indulge in that amusement, in a country which has betting shops at every corner.

It seems to me to be carrying legislation to a ridiculous extent. If, under this Bill, lotteries are very carefully supervised, are licensed and declared to be legal, I do not see why on earth they could not be referred to in newspapers or advertised. Why should they be restricted to an announcement of the result. If a charity runs a lottery which is perfectly normal, why, in the name of goodness, should there not be references to it in newspaper. It is a question of importance, for again it touches on public rights.[140]

The General Election of March 1957 returned de Valera to power. Arthur decided to contest the Seanad election held in May of that year on the Nominating Bodies sub-panel. It proved a mistake. The odds are always stacked against an Independent seeking support from an electorate uniquely tied to one political party or another. He received only 21 first preference votes and was far off the quota of 140 votes required to be elected to one of the five places available. He was one of sixteen serving Senators who lost their seats. He would have fared better had he chosen to seek election on the National University panel but this would have required a straight contest with George O'Brien. Having avoided contests in the past, there was no question of Arthur treading on his old friend's patch at this stage of their lives. Moveover, given O'Brien's popularity as a Professor in UCD and a sitting Senator, it is likely that he would have been victorious, a prospect which most certainly would not have appealed to Arthur.

De Valera did not propose Arthur as one of his nominees to the Senate in 1957. *The Irish Times* in September 1958 described Arthur as having done 'Titan's work in the Senate' and reported that many regretted that he had not been reappointed.[141]

10

Father Arthur Cox

ARTHUR'S workload continued to increase throughout the 1950s. The journey to and from Howth each day was taking its toll, not that Arthur was prepared to admit it or to adjust his lifestyle to lessen his daily burden. Eventually, he and Brigid bought one of the Irish Life Mespil Flats on Sussex Road where they frequently stayed during the week, returning to Howth at the week-ends. In 1959, they decided to sell Carraig Breac and move permanently into town. Arthur's step-daughters had long since left home. In 1952 Una married Eoin O'Malley, a doctor. In 1945 Maev had joined the Carmelite Order of nuns, an enclosed Order located in Blackrock. The normally stoical Arthur allowed himself a few tears on hearing of her decision. On the day Maev entered the convent, Arthur, in an effort to lift some of the gloom for her mother and sister, brought them to the Royal Irish Yacht Club for tea. As they stared silently into their tea cups Arthur sardonically calculated that since he had been a member of the Club for many years but rarely used it, each cup was costing an extraordinary amount of money! In the following years he was a kind benefactor of, but infrequent visitor to, the convent.

His close friend and neighbour, Henry Guinness, had served with him on the Boards of P.J. Carroll and Irish Ropes and was nominated along with him by Costello to the Senate in 1954. On hearing that Arthur was interested in selling Carraig Breac, he introduced him to Captain Mungo Park who had recently returned from Kenya and was looking for a home for his family. Park, a direct descendant of Mungo Park the famous Scottish explorer, was invited to meet Arthur in Guinness's house. They discussed everything except Carraig

Breac — from Park's famous ancestor to the transmigration of souls. Eventually, the topic of the house was raised and Arthur agreed to sell for a price which was significantly less than the valuation he had received. Mungo Park later felt that Arthur was anxious to ensure that the house would go to someone with a family who could enjoy its many pleasures and was therefore less concerned about the price he might obtain elsewhere.[142]

Arthur and Brigid set up home in an elegant establishment, no. 8 Shrewsbury Road. A large house, it was none the less significantly more manageable and convenient than Carraig Breac. Arthur's library moved with them, occupying no fewer than 140 tea chests! They did not have long to enjoy Shrewsbury Road. On 14 February 1961 Brigid Cox died. Though her family had become accustomed to her frequent illnesses, her death came as a great shock, her final illness — a stroke — occurring only four days earlier. Arthur was bereft. Despite his own great loss, his only concern was whether Brigid had been happy over the previous twenty years. He insisted that she be buried with Kevin O'Higgins.

After Brigid's death, Arthur returned to work but his heart was no longer in it. He was now approaching his seventieth birthday and while his intellect was as sharp as ever, his body was beginning to feel tired. He could easily have afforded to retire but the price of his dedication to his work over the previous forty-five years was that he had few, if any, outside interests. More importantly, he realised that the huge number of people who had come to rely so heavily on his advice would not have permitted of retirement, even if he wished it. The only way in which Arthur could make a break from his work would be if that break were absolute. The enormous void in his life created by Brigid's death could only be filled by embarking on a totally new career.

In April 1961 Arthur contacted his friend Fr Roland Burke-Savage SJ to seek his advice. He explained that since Brigid's death he had constantly thought of trying to become a priest in the evening of his days, just as Alfred O'Rahilly had already done. Arthur recalled how he had been dissuaded from joining the Jesuits when a student. He had always admired the priestly way of life from his time at Belvedere and his frequent visits to University Hall. He had been particularly close to Fr Edward Coyne SJ and had prayed with him at his final hour.

More than anything else, Arthur wished to become a Jesuit, notwithstanding the fact that the length of training was formidable, if not near impossible, for one of his age and that in all likelihood he would be required to study at the Beda College in Rome. Throughout his lifetime Arthur had been extremely religious, in the sense of having a deep interest in his religion, rather than in the sense of being overtly devout. The history of the Catholic Church and its rituals fascinated him. He was not by any means intolerant of other faiths but he held an unswerving belief in the Catholic Church. It is unlikely that he would have gone so far as to echo John A. Costello's declaration during the Mother and Child Scheme crisis: 'I am an Irishman second; I am a Catholic first,' but his Catholic beliefs were rarely far below the surface.

Fr Burke-Savage was moved by Arthur's genuine desire to become a priest and decided that he should be given every encouragement. He went to see the Archbishop of Dublin, John Charles McQuaid, to discuss the matter. The Archbishop was also keen on the idea but recognised the practical difficulties of a seventy-year-old seeking to become a Jesuit. Having thought the matter over, he suggested a compromise to Fr Burke-Savage: if Arthur could get into Milltown Park (the Jesuit Theologate in Dublin) and get professors to tutor him privately for two years, the Archbishop would gladly ordain him as a priest of the Archdiocese of Dublin and after that would willingly give him his *exeat* to join the Jesuits if he still wished to do so. Fr Burke-Savage recalls Archbishop McQuaid's reasoning for his approach: 'If he begins as a Jesuit he will be in the grave before you have him ready for ordination!'[143]

Fr Burke-Savage next approached Fr James Corboy SJ, then Rector of Milltown Park. Fr Corboy was not very enamoured with the idea of Arthur joining the community at Milltown. He was concerned that Arthur would find it difficult to adapt to the structured religious life and would not fit in with the other scholastics who were obviously much younger than he and who, by this stage, had been together for a number of years. Despite his doubts, Fr Corboy relented and agreed that Arthur could enter Milltown in October of that year.

The summer of 1961 saw Arthur busy organising his affairs in preparation for his new life. One by one his friends and clients were informed of the news. He was very fortunate that the practice could be handed over into the capable hands of Niall McLaughlin, Daniel O'Connor and Frank Scott. Arthur maintained contact with the firm even after he joined Milltown. The house in Shrewsbury Road was sold. He resigned from the Council of the Incorporated Law Society, Daniel O'Connor being co-opted in his place.

He decided to donate his library and that of his father to Milltown Park. The two collections filled over two hundred shelves in the Milltown library. Dr Cox's collection included a great deal of Irish political biography, and a copy of Yeat's first volume of poetry *The Wanderings of Oisin* which Dr Cox bought in Sligo soon after it was published. Arthur's collection was even more expansive than that of his father including, as it did, several important first editions, one being a copy of Joyce's *Ulysses,* together with editions of, among others, Dante, Cervantes, Machiavelli, Goethe, Rabelais, the Elizabethan dramatists and a large collection of books on Spanish history and art in which Arthur had a special interest.

His affairs in order, Arthur arrived in Milltown Park on 15 October 1961. He brought virtually no personal belongings with him. He was given a small room on the second floor of the Retreat House which Una did her best to make comfortable for him.

Fr Corboy's concerns about Arthur not being able to adapt were quickly allayed. The ascetic life expected of scholastics was nothing new to Arthur who had always led a spartan existence. From the beginning he insisted on being treated like all the other scholastics. He sought and received no special favours, apart from a telephone in his room so that his office could continue to contact him. He adjusted quickly to his new life. As with all previous challenges, he was determined to succeed. Each morning there were prayers in the chapel for about an hour before early Mass. One priest who, before Arthur's arrival, had been accustomed to being first into the chapel in the morning remarked to Fr Corboy that no matter how early he came down Arthur Cox was always there before him!

That Arthur fitted in so well at Milltown is a tribute to his own determination and resourcefulness but is also thanks, in no small measure, to the friendship of one particular fellow scholastic, Frank O'Neill. Fr Corboy decided that Arthur should have someone to look after him and to act as a link with the younger men at Milltown. Frank O'Neill was chosen for this role as 'guardian angel', a role he fulfilled with great devotion and understanding.

Arthur was very fortunate to have Frank O'Neill as his support and friend in Milltown. Through him he became friendly with his fellow scholastics. He also got to know a number of the older priests who were very scholarly and who were living in Milltown at the time. These included Fr Aubrey Gwynn SJ who fifty years earlier had signed his name in the Register of the new University College beside that of Arthur Cox.

Arthur did not attend lectures with the other scholastics. Instead, he was given private tuition in his room by two priests: Fr O'Grady who taught dogma and Fr Joy who taught moral principles. His faith was simple and unswerving. He could not see the reason for 'all the fuss', explaining to Frank O'Neill: 'Since God has revealed all this, I believe absolutely.' He was very orthodox in his views and had great difficulty in coming to terms with the more modern trends in theological thinking. The times were changing quickly. Vatican II was on the horizon but Arthur's view remained that theology was little more than a synonym for cathecism. Study therefore played little part in his life at Milltown.

Those who shared his years in Milltown were not really conscious that the elderly gentleman shuffling along the corridors or doing crosswords in the study was the foremost solicitor of his generation. Arthur rarely spoke of his former occupation. Instead he listened politely to the conversation topics of his new colleagues. Occasionally, he would speak of his previous life but always in a humble tone which gave no hint of how successful he had been in his professional career.

His fondest memories were of pilgrimages with Brigid to Lourdes. In August 1962 he and Frank O'Neill — now ordained — together with Una and Eoin, went on the Dublin Diocesan pilgrimage, a trip which brought back many happy memories to him.

Though determined that his entry into the priesthood should serve to make a complete break with his past professional life, Arthur remained in contact with his friends. Vincent Crowley and Dick Browne were regular visitors. Johnny Robinson called most Sundays and brought him for a drive. On other occasions Arthur would visit Una and her family or go to see Maev (who had taken the name Sister Kevin) at the convent in Blackrock. Where Arthur went, Frank O'Neill was obliged to follow, often finding that his duties included keeping the conversation with Arthur's friends going as Arthur would lapse into one of his all too familiar silences.

He continued to show generosity to his friends. To one man who lost money on a shipping venture, Arthur wrote from Milltown in September 1963: 'Unfortunately, however, the Jesuits no longer have ships. It was, I think, through having too many things of that kind that they got suppressed in the Eighteenth Century. They don't want that to happen again. Like my friends, the Train Robbers, I have, at the moment, more money than is good for me. I am taking the liberty of sending a cheque....'

In early 1962, Fr James Corboy was appointed Bishop of Monze in Northern Rhodesia. He was the first Bishop appointed to this new diocese. In geographical terms, it was approximately the same size as Ireland. The area had strong links with the Jesuits, dating back to the early part of the century when two Jesuits from the English Province made their way north from the Zambesi River and developed a mission at Chikuni. In 1927 this mission was taken over by Polish Jesuits. A college was founded, providing primary as well as secondary education, along with teacher training courses. Since 1946, however, the Communist government in Poland had prevented new Polish Jesuits from joining the Chikuni mission. With the mission in danger of collapse, nine Irish Jesuits were sent to lend their support. Two years later the number of Irish Jesuits had trebled. Throughout the 1950s the mission flourished, education inevitably being the Jesuit priority. In 1960 a formal hierarchy was established in Northern Rhodesia. Given the enormous contribution made by the Jesuits at Chikuni it was entirely appropriate that the first Bishop of Monze, which included Chikuni within its diocese, should be an Irish Jesuit.[144]

Though delighted for Bishop Corboy on his elevation, Arthur was becoming anxious about his own position. His anxiety was increased by the departure for Africa of someone to whom he had grown close and on whom he had begun to rely. In truth, Arthur had given little thought to where he would like to perform his priestly duties. His objective was to become a priest. He had not given up hope of joining the Jesuits but, beyond that, nothing was planned. Archbishop McQuaid had initially thought of Arthur being given a role as informal legal adviser to the Dublin diocese, but nothing came of this idea. While Arthur would have served wherever he was asked, such a position did not appeal to him.

By the middle of 1962 Arthur had little remaining involvement with his legal practice. Yet as long as he remained in Dublin he could never fully detach himself from his previous life. When Fr Frank O'Neill followed Bishop Corboy to Monze, Arthur's closest bonds with his new life were suddenly gone. He decided that he too should go to Northern Rhodesia. He immediately wrote to Bishop Corboy asking that he be allowed to join the mission.

Bishop Corboy, who had been concerned about Arthur surviving in Milltown, was all the more reluctant to have him face the challenges of Africa at his age. Life on the missions was primitive. Disease was an inherent risk of the job. It was essential that the priests quickly learned the Tonga language. All these factors weighed heavily against Arthur being permitted to join. The task faced by the missionary priests was daunting enough without the added burden of a fragile seventy-one-year-old. Bishop Corboy refused Arthur's request.[145] Arthur, however, was not so easily dissuaded. Letter after letter arrived to Bishop Corboy. As so often before, his persuasive skills won through. It was agreed that, once ordained, he could join his friends in Monze.

Ordination eventually came for Arthur on 15 December 1963, two years and two months after he first entered Milltown. In the last few months before ordination he had shown signs of impatience at the wait. In October 1963 he completed the full Long Retreat with the Tertians in the Jesuit house at Rathfarnham. The ordination ceremony was held in Milltown with Archbishop McQuaid honouring his commitment to ordain Arthur as a secular priest. Bishop Corboy was present for the occasion as were many of Arthur's friends from the Milltown Park community. So too were old friends like John A. Costello, Paddy McGilligan and George O'Brien, his step-daughter Una, his cousin Aileen and other distinguished guests including Sean T. O Ceallaigh, W.T. Cosgrave and James Dillon.

On the following day, 16 December 1963, Fr Arthur Cox said his first Mass in the chapel at the Carmelite Convent in Blackrock where his step-daughter lived. Arthur originally had ambitious plans for a large celebration in the Church on Westland Row to which everyone he knew would be invited. He was particularly anxious to invite all of the many Dublin taxi drivers who had driven him over the years. He was reluctantly dissuaded from this course, it being rightly considered that the ordeal of saying Mass in public for the first time was such that a smaller congregation in a more private setting would be preferable.

On 10 August 1964 Arthur left Dublin for the last time, going first to Lourdes and then to Rome en route to his new life in Africa. Many of his friends were at Dublin Airport to wish him well. Fr Frank O'Neill was returning to the missions at the same time and, as so often before, he was on hand to assist and support Arthur on the journey. Aer Lingus gave VIP treatment at Lourdes to the travelling priests and again at Rome, although the privileges stopped for the flight from Rome to Nairobi when it was discovered that their belongings were overweight! Arthur later wrote to Maev: 'Rome was wonderful. We saw a lot, but it would take years to see one-tenth of what is there. We saw the Pope twice. He does not give private audiences at Castlegandolfo. We had bad luck, because he passed with Fr O'Connell along a passage about two seconds after we had left it. From Rome, we came down at Athens. It was sad to be there, closed in the airport and to see nothing of the city. Athens is really one of the few places I have really wanted to see.'[146] From Nairobi they flew to Salisbury where they lunched with some English Jesuits before flying on to Lusaka. There they were met by Bishop Corboy and the three spent a few days in Lusaka before heading for Monze.

Arthur settled in quickly at Monze. His wonderment at all the new experiences which were bombarding him daily led him to confess: 'If I had a dictaphone, my old typists, and plenty of time I might make an effort to write you [Maev] a worthwhile letter to recount all I have seen and experienced since we left Lourdes — but, even so, unless I were a James Joyce or an Evelyn Waugh, or someone like that it would be quite useless. And fortunately perhaps I am neither.' From the start he was extremely happy: 'I am very glad I have come here. One feels it is very worthwhile and is very glad of the chance. One feels much closer to reality here and there is an enormous amount to be done.'

His first appointment was as Extraordinary Chaplain to the local convent and the new hospital at Monze which opened shortly after Arthur's arrival. The Sisters in the convent were members of the Missionary Sisters of the Holy Rosary from Killeshandra, Co. Cavan. When Fr O'Neill informed Arthur that he had been appointed Extraordinary Chaplain, Arthur, true to his old form, replied: 'Extraordinary is the word!'[147]

Shortly after his appointment to the convent and the hospital at Monze, Arthur was asked to undertake a journey of 200 miles to Namwala where, as so often had happened in the past at home, the Sisters of Charity required the benefit of his legal expertise and his business acumen to sort out a problem they had encountered in relation to the opening of their new Arthur Davison Memorial Hospital. He later carried out a review of the insurance arrangements on all the mission houses and hospitals.

Bishop Corboy tutored Arthur in the Tonga language. Although a gifted linguist, Arthur found it difficult to learn the new language and was never more than adequate at speaking it. He was conscious of its importance, reporting to Una: 'The Tonga language is a *must*. When the vernacular

Mass comes, it will be largely used. Of course the schools all speak English and anyone who has been to school knows it. But lots of people don't — especially of course the very poor. It is very difficult — or at least I find it so. In most languages you recognise words but there seems to be no connection at all here. And the philosophy is quite different. As you know, Zambesia is a very large country. Tonga is merely one of the languages. There are about six main languages. The African is very keen on Africa for the Africans. One is hopelessly handicapped when one doesn't know the language. And the people *want* things like the Prayers after Mass, or the Holy Rosary, to be in their own language.' To another friend he wrote: 'I have made representations to the Holy Ghost on the question of the Tonga language and the gift of tongues. I gather however that in the modern world one must go the hard way!'

Arthur was popular with the local people. He moved very slowly, spoke in his usual quiet tone and was very gentle, all traits which appealed to his new flock. He continued to travel, doing his private retreat at Kalomo with Father Cummins whose father had been at Belvedere with him, relieving Fr O'Neill at Namwala, helping Fr MacDonald at Kasiya, taking a 'joyride' to Livingstone to visit the Victoria Falls. Christmas 1964 was spent with Fr O'Neill at Namwala, where at Midnight Mass on Christmas Eve the priest, in keeping with the new rite, faced the people for the first time. The locals, according to Arthur, liked it. Arthur himself continued to find it difficult to come to terms with the changes which were coming rapidly to the old order. 'I don't like at all the English version of the Mass which we must use,' he explained in a letter to Una; 'It is called the "Standard Missal" and is published in Belgium. I don't know what form is prescribed in Dublin. It is a great pity that more care was not taken to keep all English speaking countries with the same text.'

These occasional complaints were very much the exception in Arthur's letters home. In his time in Africa he wrote regularly to Una and Maev and to many of his old friends and former clients. His letters were always buoyant and vital, full of good humour and of reports of day to day life on the mission. His love of animals remained unabated. He sent regular messages to Una's dogs, Ming and Chang, as always treating them as if they were able to read and write. He befriended a cat called Sally and sent home regular reports on her welfare. He was fascinated by the new species of animals and insects he encountered, reporting that 'the spiders here are *much* bigger than ours. And they seem hardly ever to spin webs. There is a big chap who lives on the ceiling of my room. He *says* he catches mosquitoes.' Mosquitoes were one new experience which Arthur did not enjoy: 'The mosquitoes are out in strength. Unfortunately, they like me more than I like them.' Of other mosquitoes he observed that 'they seem to be very much amused by mosquito nets.'

To Maev he wrote: 'I am glad to say I have not so far met a snake but I have met a number of beautiful little lizards — about 6 inches or so long — the exact image of the Fairytale Dragons. I don't think I have got any other sensational news at the moment.' The African climate and the weather were also constant themes: 'The mornings are getting to be a bit cold and chilly, but once the sun gets up, everything is bright and warm and hot again. The sun is lazy at present — he is not up till about 6 am.'

In 1964 Northern Rhodesia gained its independence and became Zambia. Arthur was very excited about the independence celebrations. 'The Independence business is rather reminiscent of 1921,' he enthused to Una. He was disappointed that the Pope who canonised a number of African Martyrs in the same week failed to say that Protestant missionaries who were killed were also martyrs, 'because they obviously were' and also feigned regret to his cousin Aileen that the Princess Royal did not call to see him! At Monze, the priests blessed the new flag amid great ceremony. Reporting on the occasion presented Arthur with an opportunity to joke about political differences, once so important, which now seemed so far away: 'Mr and Mrs Frank Aiken came to represent the Irish Government and came here. They were very nice. I suppose that, as a Christian, one is expected to forgive after about 40 years and 4000 or 5000 miles.'

He kept in touch with news at home and mourned the decision of the electorate not to re-elect his friend Paddy McGilligan in 1965. He recalled in letters to Kevin McCourt and Don Carroll their days together on the Board of P.J. Carroll: 'How superior the three of us would have been at one of the Dundalk Board Meetings if we had been told that in a few years one of us would be seated in the Control chair of Irish television, one in the chair of the Governor of the Bank, and one in the South of Africa!' But mainly, Arthur's letters concentrated on his new life and the childlike wonderment with which he allowed new experiences to envelop him.

On Tuesday 8 June 1965, Arthur set out for Namwala to relieve another Irish priest, Fr Edward O'Connor SJ, who needed to go to hospital to receive treatment for an ulcer. Fr Frank O'Neill came to Monze to collect him. They travelled in a Land Rover loaded with cement, shopping and various supplies for a school where they intended to stop en route. A teacher from the school accompanied them, as did a young catechist and two local girls. Fr O'Neill, Arthur and the teacher sat in front. Arthur and the teacher had a lengthy discussion about Irish history. At 1 o'clock they dropped the teacher and the girls at the school. The three remaining travellers decided to travel on to a Prayer House, a distance of about thirty miles, before stopping for tea and sandwiches.

About four miles from their proposed stop they suffered a blow-out of the right back tyre of the Land Rover, which skidded and turned over on the side on which Arthur was sitting. Arthur was the only one hurt. He had a bad gash on the left side of his head. Fr O'Neill, with the help of the catechist, moved him to the side of the road where he drank some tea which they had brought with them for the journey. He was partly unconscious but managed to whisper the first words of the Act of Contrition, a fact which pleased him greatly when he was told later.

An official Government Land Rover was coming from Namwala. Its driver agreed to bring Arthur to the hospital in Choma which was closer than Namwala. Fr O'Neill sat in the back with Arthur, who lay on a mattress. They arrived at Choma at about 3.50 pm. The hospital was run by the Irish Sisters of Charity for whom Arthur had such a great regard and whom he and his father had served so loyally. The doctor who attended Arthur advised that the wound was not

serious and stitched it. Arrangements were made to have him
moved back to the hospital at Monze.

On the following day, 9 June, Arthur was in good spirits.
Bishop Corboy, who was acting as Chairman of the Bishops'
Conference at the time, telephoned and was assured that
there was no need for him to travel to Choma. Arthur dictated
to Fr O'Neill a letter to be sent to Una, which read:

Dear Una,

Motor accident going Namwala 9th (sic) June. In Choma
hospital. Believe nothing serious — don't worry. Above all
don't dream of you or Eoin coming out here whatever
happens. Please give love to friends — such as Aileen, Ilene,
Forsyths, Frs. Counihan, O'Grady, Gwynn, Burke-Savage,
Kielys, George O'Brien. Tell *Irish Times* don't publish etc.
etc. All love to you and Maev and thanks for everything. (Fr
Frank writing this: I am in bed).

Arthur.

That afternoon Fr O'Neill returned to Namwala. On
Thursday, Arthur was visited by Fr O'Connor and Fr
O'Loughlin. He was in good form and, on learning that Fr
O'Connor was from Waterford, spoke at length about John
Redmond. As ever, his only concern was not to be a burden
on those caring for him. He told the Sisters that if he got the
attention in Heaven that they were giving to him, he would
go as soon as possible. He prayed silently that evening and
had a good night's sleep.

On Friday morning Arthur received Holy Communion
from Fr Carroll. At about 10.30 am, while chatting to one of
the nurses, he collapsed. Fr Carroll and Fr O'Connor were
called and administered the Last Rites. Fr Carroll left to
telephone Bishop Corboy while Fr O'Connor continued to
say the prayers for the dying. Arthur was sinking fast. At 11.20
am on Friday 11 June 1965 he breathed his last. A post mortem
revealed that he had a cerebral haemorrhage and a fracture
of the skull. Slight pneumonia had set in. He also had traces
of Parkinson's disease.

Arthur's two great friends, Bishop Corboy and Fr O'Neill,
arrived at Choma that evening. They travelled with Arthur's

remains to Monze next day where Bishop Corboy said Requiem Mass. The packed church learned of Arthur's life since he arrived at Milltown and of his brilliant career before that. He was buried that afternoon at Chikuni in the grounds of the Jesuit Retreat House. Local schoolchildren sang Tonga hymns by his graveside. His tombstone read simply: 'Fr Arthur Cox R.I.P. Died 11th June, 1965.'

In Dublin, a Memorial Mass was held in the Church of the Sacred Heart, Donnybrook, where Arthur had been baptised in 1891 and where he married in 1940. The large congregation included Chief Justice O'Dalaigh, former President Sean T. O Ceallaigh, representatives of many of the companies which Arthur had advised over the years and many of his friends and relatives who had attended his first Mass eighteen months earlier. His former partners in Arthur Cox & Co. suffered a double blow, Frank Scott dying in the same week. On the very day of Arthur's death, George O'Brien lost his seat in the Senate causing him morosely to reflect that he was now a live ex-Senator while his great rival Arthur was a dead ex-Senator.[148]

Scores of tributes arrived from clients and friends recalling his brilliance, his kindness and his gentleness. Terence de Vere White wrote in *The Irish Times:*

The tragic irony of Arthur Cox's end — its utter inappropriateness — completes the life of an extraordinary man. A brilliant student who afterwards came to the top of his profession, to retire at 70 and become a priest when a childless and recent widower — there is nothing in that raw summary of the facts to suggest the nature of the man or the manner of his life. One shrinks from the banality of describing him, as 'a character' — that expression is so readily put to use where eccentricity is unredeemed by qualities of value.

Father Cox's eccentricities were always secondary. They were accidental or at least incidental. Opinion was always divided as to the extent of self-consciousness that lay behind the dilapidation and woebegoneness of the façade. There were no two opinions about the quickness, keenest grasp, knowledge and articulateness behind it. On the surface he was shy and abstracted; and in conference he did not so much rush in to dominate as bide his time, more concerned to say the last than the first word. After he had spoken there was rarely anything left to say.

He did not brook contradiction nor care greatly to listen. Eminent Counsel used to dominating consultations, found themselves sitting at a table with clients while the solicitor in the case walked up and down behind them, setting out the facts with enviable lucidity.

He used to say that he wanted to be an artist and he left his enormous practice to become a priest when still in undisputed mastery, but his degree of dedication to his profession was unprecedented.

Apart from his cleverness, he had qualities that made him invaluable to clients. Reticence was natural to him. Loyalty was absolute. He fought like a tiger for anyone whose case he took up. And if he could 'see all round' a situation, it never blunted his presentation of his clients' case. Jealous of his honour, he was wonderfully kind in times of trouble, and an unswerving friend...[149]

From around the globe, colleagues who had known Arthur sent their respects. From Fort Worth, Texas, Luther Hudson wrote in these terms:

In the past thirty years I have covered a large part of this country and parts of a number of other countries, meeting all kinds of lawyers under all kinds of circumstances. I have never had dealings with any attorney in any country for whom I had the same affection and respect that I had for Arthur Cox. His truly outstanding intelligence and integrity I recognised and respected, but it was his kindliness, sincerity and sense of humour which I most admired and which has left me with memories which I shall always cherish.

I would like to say to your firm, to his family and to Éire that a lawyer in Fort Worth, Texas, shares their loss.[150]

The tribute which Arthur would most have appreciated came in a letter to the *Evening Herald* on 16 June 1965:

Tribute to late Rev. A. Cox

Sir — As a taxi-driver who frequents the rank on St Stephen's Green, I would like to pay our last tribute to one who endeared himself to us over many years.

Over a long span, the late Rev. Arthur Cox was very highly regarded among the people we met and drove. He continually observed all the drivers and whenever he missed one from the rank, his first thoughts were about the missing one's circumstances and family difficulties.

He would never hear of any complaint about our men on the rank; and when consulted about matters concerning our livelihood or other affairs, his advice and guidance were freely given without fee or reward.

We mourn his loss and extend our sympathy to all connected with such a kind and gentle soul. He has gone to the eternal rest and reward which he fully earned throughout his wonderfully lived life-time. May he rest in Peace. — J.J.K.

On one visit with Frank O'Neill to Vincent Crowley's house during Arthur's time at Milltown, Crowley joked that, once ordained, Arthur would only need to receive the Last Rites to have received all seven Sacraments. 'If you do, Arthur', Crowley continued, 'you'll have yet again achieved something none of your friends can match.' Perhaps the smile on Arthur's face as Fr O'Connor prayed was not only because he was going home to his God. Perhaps Arthur was recalling, with quiet satisfaction, his old friend's joke.

Notes

1.   *The Irish Times,* 14 June 1965.

2.   National Archives, Bodkin Papers 1155/1/5/1.

3.   'Michael F. Cox (1851–1926)'. A tribute by J.B. Magennis in *A Century of Service, 1834–1934, St Vincent's Hospital Dublin,* Browne and Nolan 1934.

4.   *Cecilia Street — The Catholic University School of Medicine 1851–1931,* F.O.C. Meenan, Gill and Macmillan 1987.

5.   Arthur Cox Papers.

6.   National Archives, Bodkin Papers 1155/1/5/1.

7.   National Archives, Bodkin Papers 1155/1/5/1.

8.   National Archives, Bodkin Papers 1155/1/5/1.

9.   Quoted in *Charles Stewart Parnell* by F.S.L. Lyons (pp 582–583), Collins 1977.

10.   See *John Dillon, a Biography* by F.S.L. Lyons (pp 270–272), The University of Chicago Press 1968.

11.   Monsignor Curran's Memoirs in the O Ceallaigh papers, National Library, MS 27, 278 (1), (p. 114).

12.   Arthur Cox Papers.

13.   O'Higgins-O'Malley Papers.

14.   *The Irish Times,* 22 February 1926.

15.   Quoted in *The Parnell Split 1890–91* by Frank Callanan (p. 143), Cork University Press 1992.

16.   *Modern Ireland 1600–1972* by R.F. Foster (p. 431), Penguin Books 1989.

17.   W.B. Yeats, *Autobiographies* (p. 559), quoted in *Culture and Anarchy in Ireland 1890–1939* by F.S.L. Lyons, Clarendon Press 1979.

18.   Thom's Directories.

19.   O'Higgins-O'Malley Papers.

20. *The Belvederian* 1941, quoted in *Portraits: Belvedere College, 1832–1982* by Bowman and O'Donoghue, Gill and Macmillan 1982.

21. *The Belvederian* 1909.

22. *The Belvederian* 1909.

23. Correspondence between the author and Terence de Vere White.

24. *The Belvederian* 1905.

25. *The Belvederian* 1905.

26. *The Belvederian* 1906.

27. *The Belvederian* 1907.

28. *The Belvederian* 1908.

29. *The Belvederian* 1908.

30. *The Belvederian* 1909.

31. 'Belvedere and History' by Owen Dudley Edwards, an essay in *Portraits: Belvedere College, 1832–1982* by Bowman and O'Donoghue, Gill and Macmillan 1982.

32. *The Belvederian* 1924, quoted in *Portraits: Belvedere College, 1832–1982* by Bowman and O'Donoghue, Gill and Macmillan 1982.

33. Jesuit Archives, Arthur Cox Diary 22 May 1913.

34. George O'Brien Papers in the possession of Mr John Lynch.

35. *Centenary History of the Literary and Historical Society of University College Dublin 1855–1955* edited by James Meenan, *The Kerryman* 1955.

36. Quoted in *Towards a New University: William Delany S.J. (1835–1924)* by Thomas J. Morrissey SJ, Humanities Press 1983.

37. *Centenary History of the Literary and Historical Society of University College Dublin 1855–1955* edited by James Meenan (p. 128), *The Kerryman* 1955.

38. *Centenary History of the Literary and Historical Society of University College Dublin 1855–1955* edited by James Meenan (p. 128), *The Kerryman* 1955.

39.   Quoted in *George O'Brien — a Biographical Memoir* by James Meenan, Gill and Macmillan 1980.

40.   Quoted in *George O'Brien — a Biographical Memoir* by James Meenan, Gill and Macmillan 1980.

41.   *The National Student* 1910.

42.   Minutes Books of the Literary and Historical Society, University College Dublin.

43.   *The National Student* 1910.

44.   *The National Student* 1911.

45.   *The National Student* 1911.

46.   *The National Student* 1911.

47.   *The National Student* 1912.

48.   *The National Student* 1912.

49.   *The National Student* 1912.

50.   'John A. Costello Remembers' in *The Irish Times,* 4 September 1967.

51.   *George O'Brien — A Biographical Memoir* by James Meenan (p. 35), Gill and Macmillan 1980.

52.   *Centenary History of the Literary and Historical Society of University College Dublin 1855–1955* edited by James Meenan (pp 130–131), *The Kerryman* 1955.

53.   *The Times,* 1 April 1912.

54.   *The National Student* 1911.

55.   *Centenary History of the Literary and Historical Society of University College Dublin 1855–1955* edited by James Meenan (p. 132), *The Kerryman* 1955.

56.   Jesuit Archives, Arthur Cox Diary for 1913.

57.   Jesuit Archives, Arthur Cox Diary 26 March 1913.

58.   Jesuit Archives, Arthur Cox Diary 15 April 1913.

59.   *The Irish Monthly,* January/February 1913.

60.   Jesuit Archives, Arthur Cox Diary 2 February 1913.

61.   Jesuit Archives, Arthur Cox Diary 23 February 1913.

62.   Jesuit Archives, Arthur Cox Diary 15 July 1913.

63. For an excellent account of the profession at the time see *The Legal Profession in Ireland 1789–1922* by Daire Hogan, The Incorporated Law Society of Ireland 1986.

64. *The Irish Law Times and Solicitors Journal,* Volume 50 (p. 120), 13 May 1916.

65. Arthur Cox Papers: Deed of Indemnity between Gerald Horan, Francis Elliott Scallan and Arthur Cox.

66. *George O'Brien — A Biographical Memoir* by James Meenan (p 80), Gill and Macmillan 1980.

67. Correspondence between the author and Aodhagan O'Rahilly.

68. Arthur Cox Papers: Letter dated 26 May 1917 from United Irish League to Dr Michael Cox.

69. Quoted in *John Dillon, A Biography* by F.S.L. Lyons (p. 415), The University of Chicago Press 1968.

70. Conversation between the author and Don Carroll.

71. *The Irish Times,* 24 July 1954.

72. Quoted in *The Irish Free State, its Government and Politics* by Nicholas Mansergh, London 1934.

73. Quoted in *The Irish Free State, its Government and Politics* by Nicholas Mansergh, London 1934.

74. Dáil Éireann Debates, 11 October 1922, column 1459.

75. *The Constitution of the Irish Free State* by Leo Kohn (p. 80), London 1932.

76. Quoted in *Independent Ireland* by Ronan Fanning (p. 48), Helicon 1983.

77. Memorandum dated 12 October 1923 to Major General McGrath TD from A.S. O'Muireadhaigh, National Archives, Department of the Taoiseach, S3331.

78. National Archives, Department of Finance, 596/56.

79. National Archives, Department of Finance, 596/41.

80. National Archives, Department of Finance, 596/56.

81. Quoted in *Ireland 1912–1985: Politics and Society* by J.J. Lee (p. 105), Cambridge University Press 1989.

82. *The Irish Times,* 6 September 1958.

83.   *Electricity Supply in Ireland: The History of the ESB* by Manning and McDowell (p. 18), Gill and Macmillan 1985.

84.   *Dublin Made Me* by C.S. Andrews (p. 94), Mercier Press 1982.

85.   *Dublin Made Me* by C.S. Andrews (p. 94), Mercier Press 1982.

86.   McGilligan Papers, UCD Archives.

87.   Dáil Éireann Debates, 15 March 1927.

88.   Arthur Cox Papers.

89.   O'Higgins–O'Malley Papers.

90.   Arthur Cox Papers.

91.   Quoted in *Dublin, A Traveller's Companion,* selected and introduced by Thomas and Valerie Pakenham (p. 216), Constable 1988.

92.   *The Irish Times,* 6 September 1958.

93.   *Industrial Development and Irish National Identity, 1922–1939* by Mary E. Daly (p. 85), Gill and Macmillan 1992.

94.   National Archives, Department of Industry and Commerce, TID1207/3415.

95.   See *The Footwear Industry in Ireland 1922–1973* by Jon Press (pp 69 and 70) Irish Academic Press 1989.

96.   Dáil Éireann Debates, 28 June 1934.

97.   *Industrial Development and Irish National Identity, 1922–1939* by Mary E. Daly (p. 179), Gill and Macmillan 1992.

98.   Quoted in 'John Leydon' by Desmond Roche, *Administration,* 27 (1979).

99.   O'Higgins–O'Malley Papers.

100.   *Labour* Volume 3, No. 17, September 1955.

101.   Letter in the possession of John Donnelly.

102.   *George O'Brien — A Biographical Memoir* by James Meenan (p. 185), Gill and Macmillan 1980.

103.   *Whigs on the Green — The Stephen's Green Club 1840–1990* edited by Cornelius F. Smith and Bernard Share (p. 166), Gill and Macmillan 1990.

104.   Conversation between the author and the late Terence de Vere White.

105. See Reports in *The Irish Times,* March 1948.

106. Report of the formal investigation into the causes of and circumstances surrounding the accident to the Super Constellation aircraft PH-LKY in the estuary of the River Shannon on 5 September 1954: Department of Industry and Commerce Report; copy in the Library of Trinity College, Dublin.

107. See *Oliver St John Gogarty* by Ulick O'Connor, Mandarin Paperbacks 1990, and see *Oliver St John Gogarty* by J.B. Lyons, Associated University Press 1976.

108. National Archives, File S13838, Department of the Taoiseach.

109. National Archives, File S13914A, Department of the Taoiseach.

110. *The Disciple and His Devil* by Valerie Pascal, Michael Joseph, 1971.

111. National Archives, File S13914A, Department of the Taoiseach.

112. *The Disciple and His Devil* by Valerie Pascal, Michael Joseph, 1971.

113. National Archives, File S13914A, Department of the Taoiseach.

114. National Archives, File S13914A, Department of the Taoiseach.

115. Arthur Cox papers — Press Release by George Bernard Shaw, 22 September 1947.

116. Quoted in *The Dan Breen Story* by Joseph Ambrose (pp 94–96), Mercier Press 1982, and in *My Fight for Irish Freedom* by Dan Breen (pp 205–206), Anvil Books 1964.

117. Arthur Cox Papers, December 1947.

118. *G.B. Shaw* by John O'Donovan (p. 130), Gill and Macmillan 1983.

119. Correspondence and documents relating to the Dorman-O'Gowan and Churchill case are from the Arthur Cox Papers on the case.

120. Quoted in *Chink — a Biography* by Lavinia Greacen (p. 229), Papermac 1991.

121. Quoted in *Chink — a Biography* by Lavinia Greacen (p. 230), Papermac 1991.

122. *The Irish Times,* 26 October l953.

123. Conversation between the author and Lord Shawcross.

124. Quoted in *Kevin O'Higgins* by Terence de Vere White, Anvil Books l986.

125. O'Higgins–O'Malley Papers.

126. Gazettes of the Incorporated Law Society of Ireland, 1941.

127. See *The Legal Profession in Ireland 1789–1992* by Daire Hogan, The Incorporated Law Society of Ireland 1986.

128. For this speech and a summary of the centenary celebrations see *Record of the Centenary of the Charter of the Incorporated Law Society of Ireland, 1852–1952* Cahill & Co. Ltd 1953.

129. Minutes of the Council of the Incorporated Law Society of Ireland: 13 December 1951; 31 January 1952; 3 July 1952.

130. Report of the Company Law Reform Committee, l958.

131. John A. Costello Papers, in the possession of Mr Justice Declan Costello.

132. 'Mr John A. Costello Remembers' in *The Irish Times,* 9 September l967.

133. *George O'Brien — a Biographical Memoir* by James Meenan, Gill and Macmillan 1980.

134. Senate Debates, 24 November l954.

135. *Record of the Centenary of the Charter of the Incorporated Law Society of Ireland, 1852–1952* Cahill & Co. Ltd 1953.

136. Senate Debates, 1 December l954.

137. Senate Debates, 30 May l956.

138. Senate Debates, 30 May l956.

139. Senate Debates, 16 January 1957.

140. Senate Debates, 14 December l955.

141. *The Irish Times,* 6 September l958.

142. Conversation between the author and Captain Mungo Park.

143. Conversation between the author and Fr Roland Burke-Savage SJ.

144. See *To the Greater Glory — a History of the Irish Jesuits* by Louis McRedmond, Gill and Macmillan 1991.

145. Conversation between the author and Bishop Corboy.

146. This and other letters are in the O'Higgins-O'Malley Papers.

147. Conversation between the author and Fr Frank O'Neill SJ.

148. *George O'Brien — a Biographical Memoir* by James Meenan, Gill and Macmillan 1980.

149. *The Irish Times,* 14 June 1965.

150. Letter to Daniel O'Connor from Hudson, Keltner, Smith & Cunningham, 14 June 1965, Arthur Cox Papers.

Bibliography

Andrews, C.S. *Dublin Made Me* (Mercier Press, Cork, 1982).

— *Man of No Property* (Mercier Press, Cork, 1982).

Ambrose, J. *The Dan Breen Story* (Mercier Press, Cork, 1981).

Bew, P. and Patterson, H. *Sean Lemass and the Making of Modern Ireland 1945–66* (Gill and Macmillan, Dublin, 1982).

Brady, S. *Doctor of Millions: The Rise and Fall of Stamp King Dr Paul Singer* (Anvil Books, Dublin, 1965).

Breen, D. *My Fight for Irish Freedom* (Anvil Books, Dublin, 1964).

Brown, T. *Ireland: A Social and Cultural History 1922–1979* (Fontana, London, 1981).

Browne, N. *Against the Tide* (Gill and Macmillan, Dublin, 1986).

Bowman, J. and O'Donoghue, R. *Portraits — Belvedere College 1832–1982* (Gill and Macmillan, Dublin, 1982).

Callanan, F. *The Parnell Split 1890–91* (Cork University Press, 1992).

Coogan, T.P. *De Valera: Long Fellow, Long Shadow* (Hutchinson, London, 1993).

Curran, J.M. *The Birth of the Irish Free State 1921–1923* (London, 1980).

Daly, M.E. 'Government Finance for Industry in the Irish Free State: The Trade Loans (Guarantee) Acts', *Irish Economic and Social History*, 11 (1984).

— 'An Irish–Ireland for Business: The Control of Manufacturers Acts, 1932 and 1934', *Irish Historical Studies*, 24 (1984).

— *Industrial Development and Irish National Identity, 1922–1939* (Gill and Macmillan, Dublin, 1992).

De Vere White, T. *Kevin O'Higgins* (Anvil Books, Dublin, 1986).

Fanning, R. *The Irish Department of Finance* (Institute of Public Administration, Dublin, 1978).

—— *Independent Ireland* (Helicon, Dublin, 1983).

Farmar, T. *A History of Craig Gardner & Co. — The First 100 Years* (Gill and Macmillan, Dublin, 1988).

—— *Ordinary Lives — Three Generations of Irish Middle Class Experience* (Gill and Macmillan, Dublin, 1991).

Farrell, B. *Sean Lemass* (Gill and Macmillan, Dublin, 1983).

Feeney, J. *John Charles McQuaid* (Mercier Press, Cork, 1974).

Foster, R.F. *Modern Ireland 1600–1972* (Penguin Books, London, 1989).

Gwynn, D. *The Irish Free State, 1922–27* (Macmillan, London, 1928).

Greacen, L. *Chink — a Biography* (Papermac, London, 1991).

Harkness, D.W. *The Restless Dominion* (Gill and Macmillan, Dublin, 1969).

Hogan, D. *The Legal Profession in Ireland 1789–1922* (The Incorporated Law Society of Ireland, 1986).

Holroyd, M. *Bernard Shaw, Volume IV — The Last Laugh* (Chatto & Windus, London, 1988).

Hopkinson, M. *Green Against Green — The Irish Civil War* (Gill and Macmillan, Dublin, 1988).

Jones, T. *Whitehall Diary Volume III: Ireland* edited by K. Middlemas (Oxford University Press, 1971).

Kohn, L. *The Constitution of the Irish Free State* (Allen & Unwin, London, 1932).

Lee, J.J. *Ireland 1912–1985: Politics and Society* (Cambridge University Press, 1989).

Lyons, F.S.L. *John Dillon, a Biography* (The University of Chicago Press, 1968).

—— *Charles Stewart Parnell* (Collins, London, 1977).

—— *Ireland Since the Famine* (Collins/Fontana, London, 1971).

—— *Culture and Anarchy in Ireland, 1880–1939* (Oxford University Press, 1980).

Lyons, J.B. *Oliver St John Gogarty* (Associated University Presses, NJ, 1976).

Macardle, D. *The Irish Republic* (Victor Gollancz, London, 1937).

MacManus, F.(ed.) *The Years of the Great Test 1926–39* (Mercier Press, Cork, 1967).

McRedmond, L. *To the Greater Glory — a History of the Irish Jesuits* (Gill and Macmillan, Dublin, 1991).

Manning, M. and McDowell, M. *Electricity Supply in Ireland: The History of the ESB* (Gill and Macmillan, Dublin, 1985).

Mansergh, N. *The Irish Free State, its Government and Politics* (Allen & Unwin, London, 1934).

Meenan, F.O.C. *Cecilia Street — The Catholic University School of Medicine 1851–1931* (Gill and Macmillan, Dublin, 1987).

Meenan, J. *The Irish Economy Since 1922* (Liverpool University Press, 1970).

—— *George O'Brien — a Biographical Memoir* (Gill and Macmillan, Dublin, 1980).

—— (ed.) *Centenary History of the Literary and Historical Society of University College Dublin 1855–1955* (The Kerryman, Tralee, 1955).

Morrissey, T.J. *Towards a New University: William Delany S.J. (1835–1924)* (Humanities Press, New Jersey, 1983).

Murphy, J.A. *Ireland in the Twentieth Century* (Gill and Macmillan, Dublin, 1975).

O'Brien, G. 'Patrick Hogan', *Studies*, 25 (1936).

Ó Broin, L. *Revolutionary Underground: The Story of the Irish Republican Brotherhood, 1858–1924* (Gill and Macmillan, Dublin, 1976).

—— *No Man's Man* (Institute of Public Administration, Dublin, 1982).

O'Connor, U. *Oliver St John Gogarty* (Jonathan Cape, London, 1964).

O'Donovan, J. *G.B. Shaw* (Gill and Macmillan, Dublin, 1983).

O'Neill, T.P. and the Earl of Longford *Eamon de Valera* (Gill and Macmillan, Dublin, 1970).

O'Sullivan, D. *The Irish Free State and its Senate* (Faber and Faber, London, 1940).

Packenham, F. *Peace by Ordeal* (Jonathan Cape, London, 1935).

Pakenham, T. and V. *Dublin, A Traveller's Companion* (Constable, London, 1988).

Pascal, V. *The Disciple and His Devil* (Michael Joseph, London, 1971).

Press, J. *The Footwear Industry in Ireland 1922–1973* (Irish Academic Press, Dublin, 1989).

Roche, D. 'John Leydon', *Administration,* 27 (1979).

Rockett, Gibbons and Hill *Cinema and Ireland* (Routledge, London, 1988).

Smith, C.F. and Share, B. *Whigs on the Green — The Stephen's Green Club, 1840–1990* (Gill and Macmillan, Dublin, 1990).

Valiulis, M.G. 'The "Army Mutiny" of 1924 and the Assertion of Civilian Authority in Independent Ireland', *Irish Historical Studies,* 23 (1983).

—— *Almost a Rebellion: The Irish Army Mutiny of 1924* (Tower Books, Cork, 1985).

West, T. *Horace Plunkett, Co-operation and Politics: an Irish Biography* (Colin Smythe, London, 1986).

Younger, C. *Ireland's Civil War* (Mullen, London, 1968).

Index